MW01534846

WOMEN IN ENGINEERING

Alice Posner

VGM Career Horizons
A Division of National Textbook Company
4255 West Touhy Avenue
Lincolnwood, Illinois 60646-1975 U.S.A.

Cover photo: Cynthia Coleman, Engineer.

ABOUT THE AUTHOR

Alice Posner is a professional writer. She has written extensively about women and their careers, education, and legislation. She is a member of Washington Independent Writers and the Institute of Electrical and Electronic Engineers. She is married and has one daughter.

ACKNOWLEDGMENTS

The preparation of this book was made possible by the remarkable women whose stories are here. Other people whose contributions were valuable to this work include: Dr. Michelle Aldrich and Roger Long of the Opportunities in Science project of the American Association for the Advancement of Science, Betty Vetter and Eleanor Babco of the Scientific Manpower Commission, Dorris Powers of Science Applications, Eleanor Zippo of Gulf Oil Corporation, and Marilyn Berman, Assistant Dean of Engineering at the University of Maryland.

CONTENTS

Gloria M. Faulring, Metals Division, Union Carbide Company.

INTRODUCTION

In 1977, women made up 2.7 percent of all engineers in the general work force. Because of the growing number of women in engineering school today, this figure is likely to increase dramatically in the 1980s. In 1978, women represented 12.3 percent of all college and university first-year engineering students, and 11.1 percent of all undergraduate full-time engineering students. In that same year, women composed 7.6 percent of all graduate full-time engineering students.

According to the Scientific Manpower Commission, by 1979 women were earning 9 percent of all the Bachelor's degrees in engineering, 5.5 percent of the Master's degrees, and 2.2 percent of the doctorates.

"More young women should be encouraged to consider engineering as a career if they have a natural bent in that direction," says Nancy Fitzroy, manager of Heat Transfer Consulting Research and Development Center for General Electric, Schenectady, New York. Ms. Fitzroy, herself a mechanical engineer, explains, "Engineering is one of only a handful of careers where a woman can make decisions for which outcome she is responsible and where the salary is commensurate with that responsibility. Even if she should not choose to pursue engineering as a lifelong career, she will find that it has given her invaluable understanding of the many technological problems of our modern world."

Irene Carswell Peden, professor of electrical engineering and associate dean of the College of Engineering, University of Washington, Seattle, comments on some characteristics of any good engineer. "Mechanical aptitude has little to do with suitability for an engineering career any-more. In some fields, such as mine, it won't hurt you, but it won't do you any good, either. Much of modern engineering is done in partnership with the computer, in a laboratory, or at a desk. Students who succeed in engineering school are typically good at math, intelligent, and have rather intellectual hobbies. Scientific curiosity, abstract reasoning skills, and good spatial visualization are relevant characteristics.

"In common with other professions, engineering also calls for self-discipline, emotional strength, and objectivity. One does not have to be *terribly* brilliant, however, because engineering does not require more intelligence than any other profession—just a different set of aptitudes and interests."

Most engineers would agree that engineering is problem solving. It doesn't necessarily require strength or manual dexterity. However, it does demand a particular type of thinking.

The National Society of Professional Engineers describes engineering as "the profession in which a knowledge of the mathematical and natural sciences gained by study, experience, and practice is applied with judg-ment and responsibility to develop ways to utilize economically, the materials and forces of nature for the benefit of . . . [humanity]."

They believe that every engineer must be able "to solve today's known problems, and equally important, to comprehend and invent ways to solve tomorrow's problems which are not even known today. In addi-tion, an engineer may be called upon to "analyze a complex situation involving [people], money, and machines to create the most efficient and economical design or system," and to "work harmoniously, intelligently and understandingly with other engineers as well as with scientists and nontechnical people."

"My advice to women pursuing technical careers is to enjoy," says Abby Gelles, a software engineer who is executive director of the Per-sonal Computing Society, Inc. "The field is a natural for women who are raised with an eye for creativity and attention to detail."

She adds, "Rather than problems [with discrimination], I always found my femininity to be an asset due to its uniqueness in a man's world. Also, for those who are interested in such things, the man/woman ratio does wonders for one's social life."

Most of the women whose stories are included in this book would agree with these statements and they would add at least two other reasons for a woman to enter engineering—it is fun and it is challenging.

The interest and ongoing satisfaction of dealing with problem solving situations in complex areas, and the stimulation of significant and exacting demands upon both one's intellect and stamina, present an unusually rewarding career field for women in engineering.

Overleaf: Judy G. Driggans during college worked for the Tennessee Valley Authority (TVA) where she is now employed as a solar engineer.

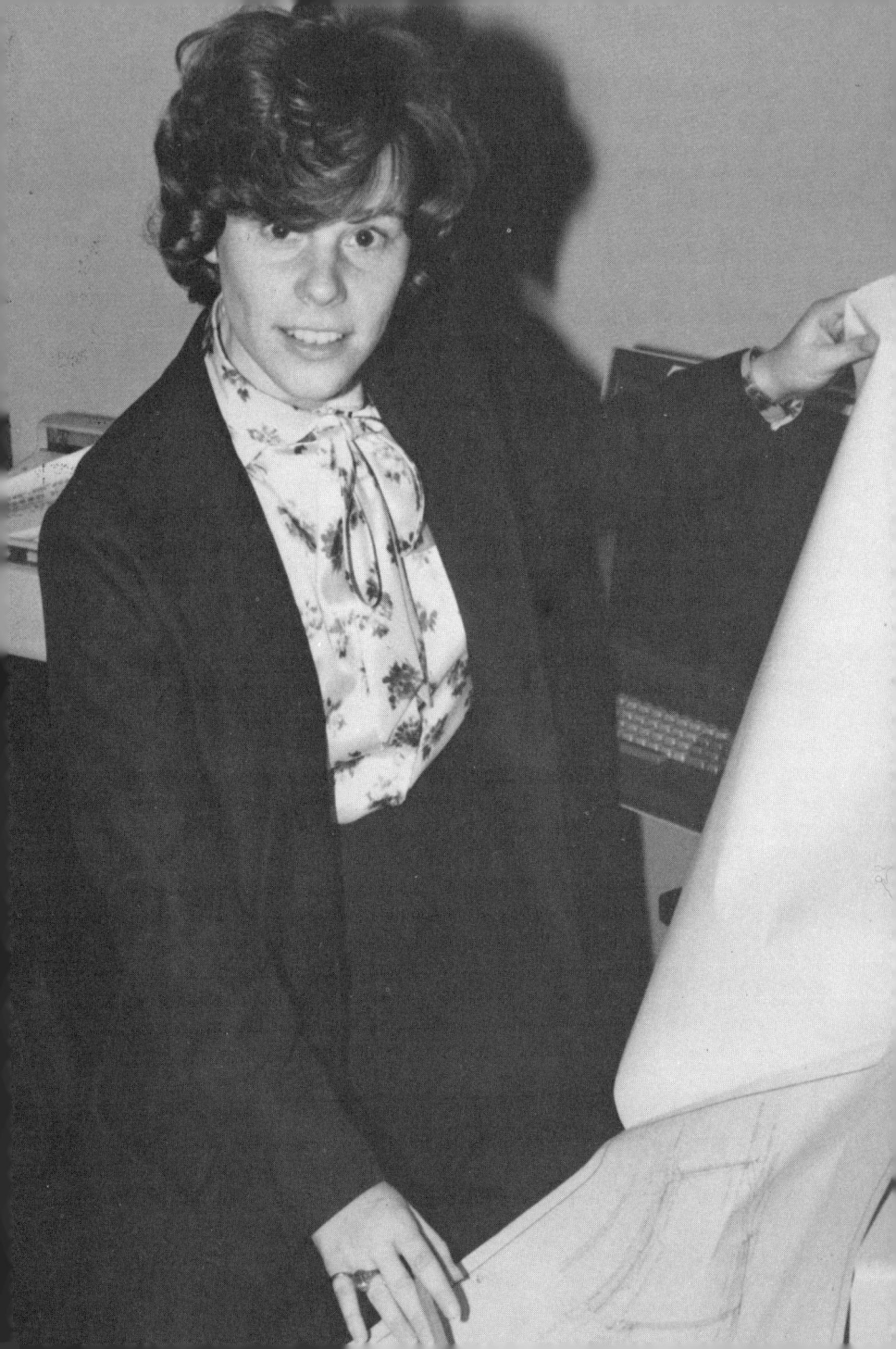

CHAPTER 1

EDUCATION AND INTERESTS

According to a study by Mary Diederich Ott, of the College of Engineering, Cornell University, women who enter engineering often differ significantly from men in several areas. Women considering a career in engineering may find that their own profiles parallel more closely those of other women in engineering, than those of the men.

In general, women often consider engineering later in their schooling than do men. Often men know by their sophomore year in high school that they want to be engineers. Many women do not make this decision until they have already entered college. This later decision may work against women, since they may not be as prepared to take engineering courses as men who knew what they wanted to do before college.

HIGH SCHOOL PREPARATION

For example, many women have not taken all the math that they can while in high school. F. Suzanne Jenniches, now developing a new system of manufacturing electrical components for Westinghouse, first began her career teaching high school biology because she did not enjoy math in high school. When she returned to school, she made up her deficiencies in math and discovered she enjoyed higher math even though she did not like arithmetic. Other women have reported similar experiences.

The math sequence is one of the critical elements in a woman's high school training if she is to enter engineering. This sequence should include a four-year program of algebra, advanced algebra, trigonometry, plane and solid geometry, and computer science.

A high school woman should have at least a grade of B in her math courses in order to enter engineering. The Ott study found that for almost half of the women math was the subject they most enjoyed in high school. However, only 32 percent of the men said that math was their favorite subject. Bioengineer Dr. Thelma Estrin believes that at least a grade of B in math is vital for a woman's success in engineering. However, some feel that a woman with a C in math could also make it.

Another requirement for those who will enter engineering in college, is to take as much of the physical sciences as possible. Many of the women whose profiles appear in this book said that their interest in engineering was kindled by courses in high school physics. However, the Ott study found that only 27 percent of the women enjoyed science most in high school as compared to 40 percent of the men.

Although engineers are sometimes stereotyped as poor communicators, none of the women interviewed for this book fit that category. All were articulate and were able to write fluently. In fact, one of the jobs of an engineer is to communicate her findings. Thus, a four-year sequence of English in high school is essential for handling courses in college, including writing papers. Such a background helps provide women with the confidence necessary to speak and write well with both colleagues and clients.

While 32 percent of the men Ott studied said they enjoyed English least in high school, only 20 percent of the women reported this. Foreign language was found to be the subject least enjoyed in high school by 27 percent of the men, and 12 percent of the women.

The Ott study found that 12 percent of the women said they enjoyed physical education least, but only five percent of the men said this. Women were less likely than men to have participated in high school athletics, or to have received physical education awards. However, many of the women interviewed for this book had an active enjoyment of such physical activities as skiing or flying an airplane.

Women who are planning to enter either science or engineering careers should take shop courses in high school. As one woman scientist explained, many young women do not get the same home experience with tools and machines that forms a common background for many boys who enter engineering. Such a course in school gives women the background and training they may not have received at home.

However, many of the women interviewed for this book reported they always tinkered with and enjoyed fixing things. Several reported that their mothers were afraid they would do things like take apart the piano. Others said they had older brothers with whom they used to work on mechanical or electrical things. Most of the women had a curiosity about the way things operated and enjoyed the challenge of discovering how things worked, so that when they malfunctioned, they could correct them.

Yvonne Y. Clark, an associate professor of mechanical engineering at Tennessee State University, Nashville, told a conference on women in engineering, "When most girls were playing with dolls, I was trouble-shooting my parents' coal-stoker furnace. Every once in a while an over-sized piece of coal would just throw the mechanism out of commission. Believe me, when it would get cold at night, my parents appreciated my skill. I was handy around the house in other ways, such as replacing worn-out cords and just keeping things in working order, or describing what was wrong when things were taken for repairs. For Christmas, I wanted an erector set, or other mechanical toys or models of anything that I could build from given directions."

Most of the women whose profiles appear in this book had a high standing in their high school classes. This goes along with the Ott study that reported more than 36% of women entering engineering had been in the top 2 percent of their high school class. Another 23 percent were in the top 5 percent. For men, the figures are 19 percent, and 17 percent, respectively. Ott also found that 73 percent of the women, and 52 percent of the men entering engineering had a high school grade average of A or A–.

CULTURAL INTERESTS

The women studied by Ott seemed more culturally sophisticated than did the men. Almost a quarter of the women reported an interest in modern art as compared to 14 percent of the men. While 56 percent of the women received a lot of pleasure from classical music, only 38 percent of the men did. Reading poetry was a pastime enjoyed by 72 percent of the women, but only 41 percent of the men.

The preferred outside reading of men and women who entered engineering differed also. More than 55 percent of the women enjoyed novels and short stories, but only 17 percent of the men did. The preferred outside reading of 11 percent of the men was science, math or engineering, but only 3 percent of the women reported this preference. Science fiction was favored by 18 percent of the men, but only by 10 percent of the women. A fifth of the men preferred reading about sports or leisure, where this reading interested only 4 percent of the women.

A recent survey of members of the Institute of Electrical and Electronic Engineers, the largest technical/professional society in the world, found that female representation in membership was 2.2 percent. The survey examined a few of the women members and found that one, Dr. Sandra Hutchins, is a collector of musical instruments. She is manager of the Signal Processing Department at ITT Defense Communications Division in San Diego. She has on display in her house a balalaika, several flutes, an organ, guitars and a child's piano built in 1860.

Another IEEE member, Jacqueline Janoski, makes a hobby of painting miniature pictures for dollhouses. Her professional work is as coordinator of computer programs at the Electromagnetic Compatibility Analysis Center in Annapolis, Maryland.

Overleaf: Marjorie Townsend has combined raising a family with the development of a successful career as an electrical engineer.

CHAPTER 2

BACKGROUNDS OF WOMEN
IN ENGINEERING

One recent survey of the background of women who enter engineering by Worcester Polytechnic Institute, revealed that most had a strong supportive relationship with both parents and a genuine respect for women in traditional occupations. Other studies have said that often women who enter engineering identify with their fathers more than with their mothers. In fact, several studies have shown that many women who enter engineering had fathers who were engineers.

Some studies have shown that engineering students tend to come out of a blue collar background. Other studies, and the experience of many of the women profiled in this book, show that the parents of women who have entered engineering tended to be more highly educated than those of men who did.

The study by Dr. Mary Diedrich Ott of Cornell University revealed that in 1976 almost one third of the women in engineering programs had fathers who were engineers. In the overall university population, only 11 percent of the women had fathers who were engineers. In both the general university and the engineering school, women with mothers who were engineers represented .1 percent of the population.

The importance attached to a college education by parents is one factor which influences women's retention in college. Dr. Ott notes, "A larger proportion of women who indicated that their parents considered college attendance extremely important were retained.

Women in the Worcester Polytechnic study also indicated that women entering engineering felt a very positive sense of femininity, and considered themselves physically and intellectually attractive to men. Most of the women interviewed for this book were interested in fashion and as a group were exceptionally attractive.

Many of the women studied were the oldest or youngest child in their families. Other studies have found that many women who enter engineering and other nontraditional careers were the oldest child in the family, or at least the oldest girl.

According to Dr. Ott, enjoyment and a sense of fulfillment played a greater role for women than status or income expectation in their career choice. She found that the opposite was true for most men.

MARRIAGE AND FAMILY

Most of the women who entered engineering, according to Dr. Ott, anticipated marriage and a family. The Society of Women Engineers found that 52 percent of their members were married, 38 percent were single, 8 percent were divorced and 2 percent were widowed. Twenty-seven percent of their members had children. Of these, 33 percent had one child, 40 percent had two children, 17 percent had three children, and 10 percent had four or more children.

Dr. J.E. (Nora) Sabadell, lecturer and member of the research staff in chemical engineering at Princeton University stated the situation this way: "Your profession has nothing to do with your femininity, your family situation, or anything else but your capability to do a good job at it. Why does a man have to be the breadwinner? If he wants to stay home and write or take care of the children, he should. Or if a woman wants to stay home and spend all her energies there, she should. But if she wants to be an engineer, why not?"

Dr. Sabadell has found a way to pursue her career. According to *The University: A Princeton Quarterly,* she is married to an engineer and they have three children who she says are proud of both their parents. The children are apparently comfortable having both parents involved with careers.

Most of the women included in this book are married and many of them have children. They recognize the demands of their jobs, along with the demands of their children. Several of them found that engineering enabled them to follow their husbands and find an engineering job wherever they relocated. However, one of the younger women wondered whether it would be possible to find a man who would agree to move to accommodate her career changes.

Another woman engineer has suggested that in a two-career family with children, either the husband has to assume the traditional wife's role or both have to share this responsibility. A few women suggested selecting a mate with this in mind. Full-time household help is another option.

Dr. Mildred S. Dresselhaus, associate department head of electrical science and engineering at the Massachusetts Institute of Technology, discussed an important factor in her success. "My husband has always been interested in furthering my career." She explains, "With his help and a faithful baby-sitter who has worked with us lovingly for twelve years, our household has been managed happily. Our children take an interest in both their mother's and father's work and are quite fascinated by the interesting house guests and foreign travel that are by-products of our careers. They have been given a great deal of independence and responsibility at an early age, and are the better for it. I would assert that it is possible to provide loving care to a family while carrying out an active professional career. Marjorie R. Townsend and Dr. Maryly Van-Leer Peck, whose stories appear in this book, had similar experiences in raising their children.

The Ott study found that women differed from men in their anticipation of marriage and children. Only 81 percent of the men studied expected to marry, while 87 percent of the women did. Over 53 percent of the men expected to have a family, but only 44 percent of the women did. Of the total women, 19 percent expected to have children and a full-time job, while another 19 percent expected to have children and a part-time job.

Men viewed women's roles differently, according to the Ott study. Five percent of the women said they wanted to stay home with their children while more than 25 percent of the men said that this would be their preference for a woman's role.

SELF-CONFIDENCE

Though women who enter engineering school on the whole tend to be brighter than men, they usually are not as self-confident about their abilities. The Ott study in 1977 asked if women expected their academic performance to be better than other women's and 26 percent said "yes." Twenty-four percent said they expected their performance to be better than men's. By contrast, 36 percent of the men said they expected their academic performance to be better than other men's, and 39 percent expected it to be better than other women's.

More than 38 percent of the women Ott questioned in 1977 said that they had no close women friends in engineering. Yet another 10 percent of the women said that female engineering students were the greatest influence on them during their freshman year.

Men in the 1977 Ott study seemed to be more aware of the ratio of women to men than were the women. While 64 percent of the men said that there was too high a proportion of men, only 25 percent of the women agreed.

Overleaf: Women and ethnic minority members are steadily increasing in many engineering areas, and in most engineering schools.

CHAPTER 3

MINORITY WOMEN

Black, Hispanic, Native American and Asian-American women are engineers. An increasing number of minority women are in engineering schools today. In the fall of 1976, Dr. Ott's study reports, black women represented nearly 5 percent of the women in engineering.

Cynthia Coleman, a black woman whose profile appears in this book, is a reservoir engineer with Exxon Company, U.S.A. She recalled that her parents opposed her entrance into engineering. "They thought I would go through four years of college and not be able to get a job." she explained. After her graduation from the University of Houston, she received many job offers.

Coleman found that college was difficult, however, because she lacked basic skills that she could have acquired in high school if someone had told her they would be needed. These included advanced math and mechanical drawing. She almost dropped out of engineering school because of a heavy load of make-up courses in addition to the regular difficult engineering curriculum. However, she is glad that she persisted and is now a professional engineer. Coleman's profile is in the section on Natural Resources.

According to Dr. Ott, the sources of support for the black and white women differed. Dr. Ott found that for white women, parents paid almost 65 percent of the costs and the rest was supplied by scholarships, Among black women, parents paid about seven percent of the costs and scholarships supplied approximately 77 percent. In both cases, loans and student work supplied the remainder.

The Opportunities in Science program of the American Association for the Advancement of Science is especially concerned with encouraging minority women to enter careers in engineering and science. They keep a register of minority women engineers, most of whom have reported experiencing more problems with being a woman than a minority group member.

One black woman, Yvonne Y. Clark, associate professor of mechanical engineering at Tennessee State University in Nashville, said that in several of her previous jobs she was the only black as well as the only woman. One of her male colleagues suggested that she wear dangling earrings under her hard hat, so the others could tell when she was coming and refrain from using offensive language in her presence.

The problems facing many minority women who enter professional careers in science and engineering are described in: *The Double Bind: Minority Women in Science and Engineering*, which is available from the American Association for the Advancement of Science.

Overleaf: Betty Platt, now a successful sales engineer with York Division of Borg-Warner, began engineering school at the age of 30.

CHAPTER 4

COLLEGE

CHOICE OF A COLLEGE

A woman considering a career in engineering faces her first obstacle in choosing a school that will meet her needs. She has a wide choice. A list of schools with engineering programs accredited by the Engineer's Council for Professional Development (listed in the appendix) is available from that group.

In considering which of these schools would be best to enter, a woman might be interested in the number of other women already enrolled. Some schools, such as Purdue University, have enrollments of 20 or more percent women. Other schools have many women on staff. This may be particularly helpful to women who enjoy contact with other professional women.

In experiments designed to encourage women to stay in school, it was found that a support group for women students decreased the dropout rate tremendously. You might check to see if the school you are considering has such a group.

FINANCIAL AID

Obviously, one of the major considerations for most people attending school is finances. Colleges are expensive, especially if the engineering program is spread over five, rather than four years. Some schools offer financial aid, but it must be applied for separately from admission. In some cases, additional financial aid may be available for women entering engineering.

The Business and Professional Women's Foundation has a special loan fund for women in engineering studies which provides for loans up to $10,000. Application deadline for this program is May 15. Send a self-addressed, stamped envelope for information to: BPW Foundation, 2012 Massachusetts Ave., N.W., Washington, D.C., 20036.

There are many other sources of financial aid. A high school guidance counselor will be able to identify the most relevant of these for you. However, it is wise also to do some research yourself. There are many scholarships and financial loan programs of which few are aware, and for which you may be eligible. For example, certain scholarships are open to you if you are the daughter of a veteran of the armed forces. If your parents are members of a service or social group, such as the Elks, or a fraternity or sorority, there may be money available for you, too. Most local libraries have copies of books listing scholarships and loan opportunities.

Some schools offer a co-op program which allows students to hold a job while attending school. Because the co-op job is usually in the field of engineering, the work experience supplements a student's classroom learning. Another possibility for income is a work-study program, where a student may work at any job and go to school. However, the amount of money which may be earned in this program is limited and the work may not have any relevance to engineering. A student with computer programming experience may be able to find part-time or temporary jobs while attending school.

However, the engineering curriculum is quite strenuous and you may need all your extra time for studying. Thus, a loan program may fit your needs better. Many women are fearful about going into debt to finance their education. This is false reasoning. If you take out a loan and go through school, you can soon be out in the work force earning more than enough to pay back the loan. Without the loan, you may waste much time working at a nonprofessional job, earning little in salary, trying to save up enough for college.

Summer employment is a way many students not only earn money, but gain valuable job experience that they later can parlay into higher paying jobs. Several of the women in this book held part-time or summer jobs. Once they earned their degrees, these jobs helped them advance in the company. One woman reported that summer employment was worth an extra $2,000 added to entry level salaries.

CURRICULUM

In the typical four-year curriculum, the first two years are spent mainly on basic science, including mathematics, physics, and chemistry and the humanities, social sciences, and English. Since these first two years are general, at least one woman suggested saving money by attending a community college for this background.

Betty Platt, a sales engineer, explained that by a attending a community college, she gained needed confidence and more personalized instruction than would have been possible at a larger institution. The last two years of college are generally devoted chiefly to engineering with emphasis on a specialty.

A student studying materials engineering as a junior at the Massachusetts Institute of Technology described what a typical week was like for her. "Courses and labs take up about twenty to twenty-five hours because each subject usually meets three or four times a week. From each subject you'll probably have one problem set which is a homework assignment. You may not be required to do them but you really have to learn the work," Pamela Jorgensen concluded. Her remarks are contained in: *Choosing a Career: Women's Work: Engineering,* by the Center for Advanced Engineering Study, Massachusetts Institute of Technology.

STAYING IN ENGINEERING IN COLLEGE

Almost a third of the women who begin engineering school do not finish it, according to Dr. Mary Diederich Ott. Dr. Ott found that the retention rate for men students was 73 percent, slightly better than that for women students. A larger percentage of the women who dropped out of engineering transferred to another college course of study.

No difference was found in the retention rate between women who were graduated from public, private, or parochial schools. However, retention was higher for women who reported doing two or more hours of homework a day in high school. This is logical because of the intensity of the engineering curriculum. Several of the women whose stories appear in this book stated that a woman who enters engineering must be highly dedicated to it.

Since engineering school is difficult and competitive, a woman's prior academic achievement is related to her retention in engineering school. In fact, Dr. Ott discovered that women who earned A's in high school were more likely to stay in engineering than were other women.

Retention rates were higher for women who planned, at a point about ten years in the future, to be married, have children and work part-time.

Since the Ott study in 1976, many women both in engineering and other fields may have reevaluated the importance to them of marriage and childrearing. Some of the younger women whose stories are included here have expressed doubts about combining marriage and a career, let alone raising children.

Overleaf: L. Cogswell, (center), is an engineer in the petroleum industry where salary levels are excellent. (Photo: Gulf Oil Photo Services, Dennis Harding)

CHAPTER 5

SALARIES

Many people are lured into engineering because it pays well. However, according to several studies, women in engineering school were generally more interested in being helpful to others or useful to society than in the prospects of an above-average income. The stories in this book of Ruth Gordon, a civil and structural engineer, and Sally Kornfeld, a petroleum engineer, bear this out.

Even though many women engineers are usually not as interested in the income as in what they can do on the job and for others, the fact is that engineers do tend to earn more than college graduates in any other field. Engineering salaries are particularly high in comparison with salaries of women college graduates in other, more traditionally women's jobs.

Most employment recruiters are actively seeking women engineers. Several of the women in this book reported receiving a flood of offers from many companies and having the opportunity to choose among competing firms. In part, this is because of Equal Employment/Affirmative Action guidelines that require employers actively to seek out women and minorities for employment.

Partially in response to this, the recent salary offers made to new women engineers in some cases may be slightly higher than those made to comparably educated men. Once she has been hired, however, a woman may not receive promotions or salary increases as quickly as a man. This condition persists in some companies, despite the examples of exceptional career advances of many of the women in this book.

In 1978, salaries offered to students who had just graduated from an engineering school ranged from a low median offer of $13,450, for those who entered state government, to a high median of $17,450, for those who entered research and development. In 1978, engineering school graduates who entered manufacturing industries earned a median salary of $16,000, while those entering federal government positions began at a median of $15,800. A median salary of $15,450 was offered to engineers who entered local government.

After five years of experience in the profession, engineering school graduates commanded salaries ranging from $15,100 for those in education-research at a university, to $21,000 for people in manufacturing industries, according to 1978 figures. After about 10 years, salaries were generally above $25,000; and after 20 years, they climbed to more than $30,000, according to the Engineering Manpower Commission of the Engineers Joint Council, *Professional Income of Engineers, 1978.*

In June, 1979, engineers received the highest salaries of any of the graduating class of bachelor's degrees, reports the College Placement Council. Ranked one and two were offers for petroleum engineers, averaging $23,748 a year, and offers for chemical engineers, averaging $21,480 per year.

Salaries differed based on geographic area. The South Central United States paid beginning engineers the highest salaries, a median of $16,450 in 1978. The Mountain Area, North Central and Mid Atlantic paid about $400 less than this. The South Atlantic region offered beginning engineers the lowest pay. Median starting salaries there were $15,400 followed by the New England area where the median starting salary offered engineers was $15,500. However, within five years, much of this regional discrepancy had vanished, with all regions paying engineers a median salary of $20,000 or more per year, the Engineers Joint Council noted.

Salaries also varied greatly based on employment group and supervisory status. In all fields, supervisors received at least 25 percent more than those they supervised. In most areas, the percent difference between supervisors and nonsupervisors was more than a third and in some cases close to 50 percent, according to 1978 figures of the Engineers Joint Council.

In 1978, research and development supervisors earned a median salary of $38,050, while nonsupervisors earned a median salary of $26,650. Petroleum supervisors earned a median salary of $37,450, while nonsupervisors earned a median salary of $26,050. In aerospace, supervisors earned a median salary of $35,250, while nonsupervisors earned a median salary of $26,700. In chemicals, the median salary the supervisor earned was $32,600, while the median salary of the nonsupervisor was $25,750.

In 1978, in the electrical and electronic industry, supervisors earned a median salary of $37,100, and nonsupervisors earned a median salary of $25,900. In local government, supervisors earned a median salary of $29,250, while nonsupervisors earned $7,000 less. In the federal government, supervisors earned a median salary of $35,800, while nonsupervisors earned a median salary of $28,000. The median salary for construction and mining supervisors was $32,700, while nonsupervisors earned a median salary of $22,500.

In 1978, in utilities and services, there was a $7,000 differential between the supervisor and the nonsupervisor with the median wage for supervisors at $30,300. The largest discrepancy was in design, consulting, and engineering services, with supervisors earning a median salary of $32,500, and nonsupervisors earning a median salary of $21,850. In the mechanical industry, the median salary breakdown for supervisor and nonsupervisor was $29,400 and $21,350, respectively. In the metals industry, supervisors earned a median salary of $28,750, while nonsupervisors earned a median salary of $20,750.

These figures on supervisory and nonsupervisory positions are important, because many women who have entered engineering have not sought supervisory roles or included them in their career plans. Being a supervisor not only means more money, it also means having a say in at least some facets of corporate or government policy. See the stories of Naomi McAfee and F. Suzanne Jenniches for a description of how women can gear themselves for roles in management.

The level of educational attainment also makes a difference in the salary an individual receives. Women who enter engineering from the sciences, without an engineering degree, earn less than people who have gone through engineering school. This discrepancy persists throughout their careers. Several women have remedied this deficiency by going back to school and earning a Master's degree in engineering. One of these was Gloria Faulring, a metallurgical engineer, who also went on to get her Ph.D. Janet Embrey, who works with thermal batteries, admitted that if she moves out of her field into another area of engineering, she would probably have to go back to school.

In most fields it is not necessary to have an advanced degree beyond the Bachelor's. However, people who do go on to earn advanced degrees generally find it to be financially worthwhile.

In 1978, the median salary for a person with a Bachelor's degree in engineering and one year's experience was $16,800. This rose to $18,150 for a person with a Master's degree, and to $22,250 for a person holding a Ph.D. This differential remained throughout an individual's employment, with Ph.D's earning more than $6,000 more per year than people with only a Bachelor's degree.

The Society of Women Engineers surveyed their members and found the following things about salary. Their sample is based on responses of 1,001 fully qualified women engineers who reported gross income from their engineering positions in 1977.

The average income in the total sample was $19,020. Contrary to the high figures quoted previously, the majority of the women earned less than $15,500 in 1977. In fact, 9 percent of the woment earned less than $10,499. However, 13 percent earned more than $25,500 in 1977.

As was shown before, graduate degrees seem to improve a woman's salary level. More than 57 percent of those women who earned more than $20,500 in 1977 had a graduate degree. Only 16 percent of those earning less than $15,499 in 1977 had earned a graduate degree.

The survey of the Society of Women Engineers also showed a relationship between salary and experience. Of those women earning less than $15,499 per year, 85 percent had less than five years experience.

Among those earning more than $20,500 per year, only 22 percent had less than five years experience.

SALARY BY MARITAL STATUS		
Thousands of Dollars	% of Married Women	% of Single Women
Less than 5.5	3%	2%
5.5–10.49	4%	11%
10.5–15.49	13%	19%
15.5–20.49	39%	42%
20.5–25.49	18%	10%
25.5 and up	13%	11%
No response	10%	5%

The average salary for respondents who have children and are employed full-time in engineering was $22,119. The average salary for respondents who do not have children and are employed full-time in engineering was less, at $18,545.

The Society of Women Engineers' survey of 1977 earnings of women engineers also tabulated the median salaries of women working for four major categories of employers. Women in private industry earned a median salary of $19,078; those in utilities earned a median salary of $19,840; those in civilian jobs with the federal government earned a median of $20,404; and those in colleges or universities earned a median salary of $18,453. However, caution should be exercised in relying upon these figures because of the small number of respondents in categories other than private industry. The reader should also be aware of the impact of a shortage of engineers and inflation on current salaries offered to both women and men.

Overleaf: D. Trehern, engineer. (Photo: Gulf Oil Photo Services)

CHAPTER 6

PROBLEMS TO MEET IN
ENGINEERING CAREERS

While most of the women whose stories are in this book love their profession, they admit to having problems. They advise young women to learn about these before making up their minds to be engineers.

LONG HOURS

Most frequently mentioned is the need for dedication to the field and to a professional career. Engineering is not a course of study that one can enter and still engage in multitudinous extra activities while in school. Julie Smith, whose story is included here, did manage to hold several elective offices in her school, but most women recall continuous long hours of studying and working on problems. They admitted readily that engineering is very hard work.

The second point often made about the field was that engineering is not done in isolation. Generally one works for a large organization and as part of a group, in which every member effects every other. People who enjoy solitary work should probably not enter engineering. They might do better in research science, one of the women noted.

COMPETITION

Engineering is a very competitive field. A shy wallflower will not be able to advance in her career. The competitiveness of the field requires that engineers who get ahead in their work must be the first ones with new ideas, new research, and new applications. Often to remain competitive, an engineer will change jobs frequently. In engineering, in contrast with other fields, job changing is expected. A person who does not make a job change after a few years is often thought to be in a rut. Each change requires selling yourself, either to the management of your present company, so they understand your worth and promote you, or to another company. This requires being assertive. You must not only do your job well but you must let others know that you have done a good job. One woman, whose work was going unrecognized, used the route of professional associations and publication of articles to let the rest of the community know what she was doing.

SEXUAL DISCRIMINATION

Sexual discrimination in the engineering profession is real. Even though it is against the law, it still occurs. One woman reported being shocked when she discovered that all the professional women were earning substantially less than the professional men doing similar jobs in the same office. Many young women coming out of college are surprised when they encounter discrimination in a job.

Many of the male managers are middle-aged or older and are not used to working with professional women. Several women reported that men intentionally put roadblocks in the way of their careers, by denying them earned promotions. In all the cases we studied, the women stood up for their rights and eventually got the promotions. They often wonder, however, what higher position they might have attained had they not been women.

Several of the women whose stories are included in this book were told that "We do not hire women as engineers." Many of these women, graduates of engineering schools, were told they could be hired as secretaries. Yet they persisted and are now practicing engineers in the commercial and industrial fields of their choice.

Dorris Powers now manages an engineering consulting firm with her husband, a retired major general. When she was graduated from Purdue University with a degree in aeronautics, she was told that because she was a woman, she couldn't be considered for a position as an engineer. Reluctantly, she took a secretarial job, but she taught flying and ground school on the side.

Her daughter, who is earning her bachelor's degree in electrical engineering from the University of Colorado, should not face these same problems, she commented. Her daughter is planning to work in international sales for an electrical or electronics firm.

Some men still believe that women do not belong in engineering and may go out of their way to see that women do not succeed. Women who enter engineering must see these problems as hurdles that they will overcome, and that will make them stronger for the experience.

To be sure of getting the promotions and opportunities that are her due, a woman may still have to work harder and be brighter than a man. Several of the women in this book reported that when thrown a curve or problem, they found another way to tackle the situation that in the long run, was better. The optimism and drive of the women in this book was quite strong.

Ms. Powers said that the big problem young women face is moving up in the corporation once they are hired. She bases this on the feedback she has received from many sessions of the Society of Women Engineers. "An engineering degree will open the door, but actual on-the-job experience may be far different from experience in school," she said. In an article in *Civil Engineering,* May, 1979, Ann Seltz-Petrashi explained that, "Along with facing the usual problems of adjusting to a new environment, as a 'green' engineer low on the pole, many women find they are often an object of curiosity," she wrote.

Many women reported that the pressures were often subtle but very real. In fact, several of the women in this book found it easier to deal with blatant discrimination that was out in the open than with the subtle kind. Petrashi also quotes one woman who explained, "With new people, especially, before any serious discussion can begin, we must go through the 'lady engineer routine.' Dealing with the stream of girl jokes can be taxing."

A woman may have problems not only with her supervisors but with her coworkers. According to many women in civil engineering, some men may try to test out women engineers in the field. Once the women prove their competence, however, the crews seem to accept them and follow their directions.

An additional problem may stem from the secretaries in the office. One woman said that the office secretary was one of her most formidable problems. The secretary had never dealt with a woman engineer and did not know how to treat her. She had been a mother figure to the male engineers, but she could not intereact this way with a woman.

Most women suggested that if you don't seek out problems and look for discrimination, you can succeed.

However, most agreed that there may also come a time when you must speak up about problems. One woman was doing a good job at her company but did not speak up about the minor barbs and sexual innuendos. She found she finally had to quit the job because the pressures were increased, not lessened, and became more than she wanted to take.

Another problem women mentioned was that many clients did not realize that the woman they were talking to over the phone or in an office was an engineer. They automatically assumed she was a secretary. However, they said, this was a minor annoyance.

One woman said that her boss enjoyed having her on the staff because he would take her to meetings with clients who were known to be verbally abusive. When the client saw a woman, he toned down, and the meetings were able to go on quite amicably. However, she chalked this up to being a professional and expecting to be treated as a professional.

A recent article in the *Wall Street Journal* said many women executives face problems when traveling. These may include finding ways to stop unwanted advances that men may make in planes or in bars or restaurants. One of the young women in this book suggested wearing a gold wedding band when traveling.

Travel on a job may pose a special problem to women with children. Several of the women who have raised children while pursuing their careers had full-time household help. This enabled them to participate in the company business and attend necessary conferences and late evening meetings.

Petrashi, writing in *Civil Engineering*, summarizes the advice of the women civil engineers she interviewed in these seven suggestions.

1. Get field experience and as many different kinds of engineering experiences as possible.
2. Then, head for management. That often means extra courses or a full MBA program, but it is the only way to break into upper management.
3. Join professional societies and get involved. You can meet people and gain visibility.
4. Move around and work in different firms. Women have a harder time than men working their way up through a firm over a 20-year period, and are more likely to get stuck in middle management.
5. Don't be afraid to be assertive. Make an effort to use humor when dealing with co-workers whose "jokes" may be tiresome.
6. Take responsibility. Show initiative. Women still must work harder than men to prove competence.
7. Watch out for over-protectiveness from others.

UNEMPLOYMENT

Right now engineering is a glamour field with more opportunities than most other fields. Yet, engineers too have spells of unemployment, particularly those engineers who are narrowly trained or who are unwilling or unable to relocate where there might be jobs.

In 1976, the unemployment rate of male engineers with a bachelor's degree was 3.3 percent. The rate was higher for women with a bachelor's degree. For men with a master's degree, the unemployment rate was 1.5

percent, but again, was higher for women, according to the National Science Foundation. In 1977, the unemployment rate of engineers with a Ph.D. was .6 percent for men and 3.0 percent for women, according to the National Research Council. The Society of Women Engineers paints a bleaker picture of unemployment and underemployment of its members. The first tabulation shows the number of years women reported being unemployed. The second tabulation represented the number of years the women were employed in nonengineering jobs. Rearing children at home was considered nonengineering employment by some women, while others considered it as unemployment. As a consequence, the percentage of women engineers who were job seeking is somewhat lower than the number unemployed.

YEARS UNEMPLOYED FOR WOMEN ENGINEERS

Zero or none reported	57%
1 to 5 years	29%
6 to 10 years	7%
11 to 15 years	4%
16 or more years	3%

YEARS EMPLOYED, NOT IN ENGINEERING

Zero or none reported	75%
1 to 5 years	16%
6 to 10 years	4%
11 to 15 years	3%
16 or more years	2%

Source: *A Profile of the Woman Engineer,* Society of Women Engineers, 1978.

TOKENISM

Cynthia McCarthy, a civil engineer for the Massachusetts Port Authority (Massport), describes the hazards of getting a job in *Women's Work: Engineering,* published by The Massachusetts Institute of Technology.

Prior to 1970, it was a problem just getting an appointment for an interview. When she reentered the job market in Boston in 1970, she said, "I had my choice. But for the first time I encountered 'tokenism.' I had to be careful to see if a position was being offered by a company advertising its 'liberalness', or if, in fact, professional engineering help was needed and some of the responsibility for it would be delegated to me."

Massport, where she settled, "appeared to me to be a vital organization, which relied upon the judgment and capabilities of its engineering department," Ms. McCarthy said. "They were too busy to permit the vegetation which accompanies tokenism. In addition, I was also allowed the opportunity to spend as much time in the field (on construction) as my work load permitted."

Many women feel quite wary about being hired because they are women. They know that they have worked hard and want to be hired because they are good.

One of the subtle ways in which discrimination still occurs is in the assignments women receive once they are hired. Many women get channelled into administration rather than hands-on work, which is where most rising engineers begin. From hands-on work, engineers learn about the field on the construction sites and later can bring this knowledge into management. Entering administrative positions too early may be a way to short circuit a woman's career.

Overleaf: Electrical engineer Naomi McAfee manages a $600,000,000 budget and staff of more than 250 engineers.

CHAPTER 7

ELECTRICAL ENGINEERING

According to the Bureau of Labor Statistics, electrical engineers compose the largest group of engineers—more than 300,000. Each year an additional 12,800 electrical engineers are needed.

Electrical and electronic engineering deals with the design, development, construction, installation, and maintenance of electrical and electronic systems.

Areas of interest include telecommunications, radio, radar, satellites, space travel, transportation systems, automatic/adaptive control methods, information theory, analog and digital computers, lasers and masers, solid state electronic components, fuel cells, power transmission and generation systems, and medical electronics [see bio-medical engineering section of this book].

In one exciting book, *I'm Madly in Love With Electricity and Other Comments About Their Work by Women in Science and Engineering,* women engineers and scientists describe their positions. This book, by Nancy Kreiberg, is available for one dollar from the Lawrence Hall of Science, University of California at Berkeley.

Sharon Okonski, power engineer for the National Aeronautics and Space Administration (NASA) Ames Research Center in California, described her work in this publication. "What I like best about power engineering," she said, "is working in the field—crawling in and out of

41

man-holes, working with big pieces of machinery, working with tradespeople. Also, the danger of electricity is very exciting.

"Many of my projects are involved with energy conservation, such as HVAC (heating, ventilating, and air-conditioning) systems that provide central automatic remote control of each building's environment.

"My job is to make the changes in each building to include the HVAC controls. Documentation is poor, so I am required to go into the field and trace wires to find out exactly what the wiring is and document that to include the HVAC controls. I then guide an electrician to install the controls, have the drawings put on computer magnetic tape, and tie the controls into the central computer. There are forty buildings that will be equipped with this system," Ms. Okonoski reported.

Electrical engineers are highly versatile. Because of the wide diversity in positions and backgrounds of women in electrical engineering, this section includes profiles of two women.

Marjorie Townsend, who is also profiled in this section, is responsible for the satellites designed and launched by the Goddard Space Flight Center of the National Aeronautics and Space Administration. Ms. Townsend presents a picture of a woman in a high federal government position.

Naomi McAfee is a Westinghouse executive who supervises more than 300 engineers in defense systems engineering.

She presents the story of a woman who has risen through the ranks of a large corporation.

The movement of women into electrical engineering has been slower than their entrance into other engineering disciplines. However, this is gradually changing.

In fall of 1978, women made up 6.5 percent of all electrical engineering undergraduates. Among engineering students, more than 21 percent of all men and more than 12 percent of all women chose electrical engineering according to *Engineering and Technology Enrollments, Fall, 1978,* prepared by the Engineering Manpower Commission. In 1968, according to Dr. Ott, only 8 percent of women in engineering chose electrical engineering.

MARJORIE R. TOWNSEND

Electrical Engineer

Marjorie Townsend has a role in all satellites to be launched by the Goddard Space Flight Center of the National Aeronautics and Space Administration (NASA). She is manager of the preliminary systems design group at the Goddard Space Flight Center in Greenbelt, MD. The group which she directs is responsible for all of Goddard's space hardware and ground system studies required for future missions.

"Every future mission of Goddard passes through our hands," she explains. "We determine its feasibility. This may mean the design of spacecraft, the decision on how to get into orbit, or work with scientists to help them evaluate proper instruments. Then we determine the view angles of the instruments and the best way to care for the satellites."

Originally, Townsend's group had responsibility only for spacecraft systems. As the team proved its worth, it was given more responsibilities. Today, it is the only complete systems group at the Goddard Space Flight Center. Its responsibilities include free-flying spacecraft and associated ground systems, plus Spacelab payloads.

"As manager of a newly-created group, I was able to select its members and coalesce them into a close-knit working team whose output is creative and highly productive. The group works simultaneously on a large variety of missions in space and terrestrial applications and in space sciences.

"For example, some of the problems we must deal with involve the cold outside the satellite and the heat inside the craft itself—the earth below and the sun above. For a spacecraft in a usual orbit around the earth, night occurs about every 100 minutes and lasts about forty minutes. Day lasts about an hour. We have to plan the type of heating and cooling systems that will work best in this situation.

"We are performing many space shuttle experiments," Ms. Townsend explained. Her group will help make the use of the shuttle a reality. "The shuttle will mean more freedom for people in space," she said, "and will also be used as the first stage of a launching vehicle.

"We take a satellite up on a shuttle and put it into space, and then it is on its own. We torque (point) it in the right direction and may make corrections to this by gas jets or by electro-magnets, which we can adjust. The satellite can talk to itself and to us, through radio-linked telemetry.

"The telemetry provides us with bits of data that the computer turns back into measurements. We then calibrate these data into information the scientists can use," she explained.

Currently her group is studying a mission to monitor the activity of the sun and the amount of energy it emits. "Such studies will provide more information to help us understand the weather," says Townsend. She predicts that during the next twenty years, we will more accurately understand the cause and effect relationship of the weather. In the 1980s there will be a number of satellites which will study the sun's activity plus the earth's magnetosphere and its upper atmosphere. She hopes the information from these satellites will enable scientists to correlate causes and effects of the weather. So, while everybody talks about the weather, NASA is trying to do something about understanding it.

Management

Townsend's managerial skills are as vital as her technical expertise. She must motivate people to do their jobs and then see that work is done so that it meets government requirements.

She believes this requires team building and organizational development. She was selected to attend a course given by the Federal Executive Institute. "This helped me put into words what I had done intuitively," she reports. "This seven-week training course helped me turn the looking glass on me. It emphasized interpersonal relationships.

"When I began my position as manager of the preliminary systems design group, I took my staff on a retreat for three days. We learned how we all functioned and related to each other. Based on this retreat, we decided not to include one of the people we took because he was hostile throughout the training. This experience helped us learn to know and trust each other and be able to work together. We like and respect one another. The people in our group are bright and outgoing, not dormant or passive. If we fight, it is okay if we come out friends in the end. We have no in-fighting.

"To help us maintain this, we have a psychologist come in two or three times a year and the staff learns it is okay to tell me and the others what we are doing wrong. This clears the air and keeps petty things from getting in the way. It works well. It is tiring to go through this process, but it is worth it in the end. We can get things done," Townsend emphasized.

"Working for the government is different than working for private industry," Townsend said. "In the government, you must, of course, work within a budget, but the use of staff is quite different. We can do all the experiments that we have the staff for," she explained.

In addition to managing the technical aspects of projects and the creative people who design or run them, she must be an expert in the financial arena, too. To help her understand finances, she took three courses in accounting and financial management. She already knew much of the material based on her previous experience managing projects and figuring out budgets.

She has had many other duties as well. At one point she was the leading narrator in a television show explaining telemetry and the early design of flights. Originally made for public television, it was later carried by commerical television.

For nine years prior to taking her current position, she was manager of the Small Astronomy Satellites Project. As a project manager, her responsibilities included overall project planning and evaluation, with responsibility for system design, development, fabrication, integration, and testing of the spacecraft, instruments and allied ground support equipment (computers, for the most part). After launch, as the manager she was also responsible for data evaluation and analysis reporting. In addition, she managed the financial and personnel budgets for the entire project.

In describing this project, Ms. Townsend explained, "From earlier sounding-rocket experiments which took a quick look at the stars, scientists discovered stars emitted x-rays. This justified the use of a satellite to survey the heavens for x-ray emitting stars. From 'Uhuru' (SAS-1) launched in 1970, we discovered a black hole which emits no light but sends out x-rays." The result of the first satellite which Townsend managed was a catalog of more than 400 stars which are x-ray sources.

This project presented political, technical, and personal problems which Townsend had to address. On the day scheduled for the launch of the first satellite, from the San Marco Equatorial Range in Africa, Kenya was to celebrate its independence day. Major celebrations were planned which would tie up the leaders of Kenya. Rather than hold back the launch, which would have been extremely difficult, Townsend decided that the celebrations could be combined by renaming the satellite. The SAS-1 became the *Uhuru,* which in Swahili, the major language of Kenya, means *freedom.*

Prior to the launch something appeared to be wrong with the satellite. Townsend's immediate superior wanted her to make a major overhaul of it. Instead, she recalculated. "I was right. The satellite worked like a charm in orbit," she relates. However, her boss felt that she was insubordinate and did not want to see her promoted from her government service position of GS-14 to GS-15. This was despite the fact that all other project managers already held GS-15 status. However, the director of the Goddard Space Flight Center was at the launch, saw how she had performed and insisted that she be given the promotion.

The lesson Townsend drew from that experience was that if you are sure you are right, you have to stand by your convictions.

Before becoming project manager, she was a technical assistant to the chief of the systems division. This was a staff position. She helped establish division policy and served as a consultant to the French on their satellite program.

From 1959 to 1965, she held increasingly responsible line positions in electronic design. The engineers and technicians under her direction and supervision increased from one to twenty-two engineers and ten technicians. During this time, she was personally responsible for the development of the ground-processing equipment for the infrared experiment on board the Nimbus satellite. She was also responsible for the beacon transmitter flown on the Nimbus series of satellites. Her group was responsible for the design and development of electronic instrumentation flown on the Nimbus and the Orbiting Geophysical Observatory Satellites. During this period she developed the concept for the Digital Telemetry System, for which she later received a patent.

Prior to coming to NASA she worked at the Naval Research Laboratory where she was gradually promoted from a GS-5 to a GS-12 position. Here she gained professional experience in anti-submarine warfare and underwater target detection and classification.

For eight years she held increasingly responsible positions doing basic and applied sonar research. She developed sonar processing devices and evaluated sonar techniques and display methods. She was responsible for the development of a complex frequency multiplication system using a magnetic tape recorder. She designed a new submarine detection and classification technique and a sonar simulator.

While finishing up college, she worked at the National Bureau of Standards, in Washington, D.C. She measured the radon content and breath samples of radioactive solutions. "This nonprofessional job fed us and paid the tuition," she explained.

Townsend's work helped put her husband through medical school Today he is an obstetrician. "Ironically," she noted, "I have spent all my life working with men and he has spent all his life working with women. However, we have a common interest in the sciences."

Early Experiences, Education and Family

Marjorie Townsend grew up as an only child in Washington, D.C. Her parents took her everywhere with them. She was graduated from a public high school and began college at George Washington University, in Washington, D.C., at the age of fifteen.

Her father was an engineer and because she identified with him, she chose an engineering career. She reasoned that engineering offered her a combination of math and physics which she liked, without history, which she disliked.

"I chose electrical engineering," she said, "because my father thought that my job would be working behind the scenes in television, which was a new field when I was in school. Generally, though, I realize electrical engineering was a good choice because consistently, there are more opportunities for electrical engineers than for other types of engineers," she said.

When she was eighteen, during her junior year of college, she got married and decided to work during the day and attend school at night. So, her "last year" took her three years at night school.

"Because I was young, and looked even younger, the teachers looked upon me as a younger sister. When I started college in 1945, most of the men had been in the service and were more mature. This made a difference," she declared. "I really have had no problems in school because of being a woman. In fact, I was the first woman to graduate from the George Washington University Engineering School."

Being a mother while working full-time was not so much a problem, as it was an exercise in careful time management. For the births of each of her four sons, Townsend planned her maternity leave during the thirteen days sick leave and twenty days annual leave time the government provided. Having the same housekeeper for twenty-seven years also has helped her to keep a stable home atmosphere.

"In addition," she relates, "the children learned to do chores early so they all helped out. For example, when one son was ten, he was entrusted with doing all the grocery shopping for the family. Our children had credit cards at age twelve and checking accounts at age sixteen. They learned how to wait and save up for things they wanted." Ms. Townsend believes that these traits are vital for any mature and professional person.

Other Activities and Thoughts

"I am embued with the work ethic. I have little time for relaxing," she confessed. "This year, while watching television, I made five afghans and many dresser scarves. " She also does the accounting for her husband's medical practice because "the fancy, high-priced firm he used was always late and made mistakes, and I knew I could do at least as well as they could and be on time with it. "

She also has time to be active in professional societies. She has been president of the Washington Academy of Sciences, and is active in the Institute of Electrical and Electronics Engineers. She also serves on the D.C. Council of the American Institute of Aeronautics and Astronautics, as well as the Joint Board of Science and Engineering Education. In addition she is a member of the Board of Registration for Professional Engineers for the District of Columbia.

Townsend is able to achieve so much because she attacks problems, both in engineering and personal life, in a logical step-by-step way, based on the principles learned in her training and on inherent common sense.

Sexual harassment is something Townsend does not consider a problem for herself. "Any propositions I have had, I took as kidding or teasing and turned them aside," she said. "Others have taken them more seriously. You have to be able to judge the situation clearly. For example, one of my bosses draped his arm over my shoulder to inspect my work but he did it with all the men, as well, so I did not see anything wrong with it, and did not make a big deal about it," she explained.

Currently, there is a women's group at Goddard but there are few women mentors. "I have never had anyone to talk to," Ms. Townsend admitted.

Nevertheless, she can point to three men who made a real effort to promote her career. One of her bosses once put his job on the line to give her an opportunity. "Yet, many people thought someone else was doing my work because they did not believe it was possible for a woman to do such bright things," she recalls. Two men made a real effort to inhibit her career, but she succeeded in spite of them, though she admitted, "It was often difficult. "

Townsend recalled analyzing a personal problem related to her career. "When I was sitting in Africa at the launch of my second satellite, I was depressed and did not know why. Finally, I thought about it and it occurred to me that I was not learning any more. Just like rice, which I disliked because it has no flavor, I discovered you have to learn how to modify it or accept it." She thus realized that she needs to be constantly learning new things to be happy.

Townsend is keeping her options open for the future. She says, about her job, "There is not a better job to have at Goddard than the one I have. This is a fun job. I have been able to surround myself with very bright, very stimulating people; we keep learning. This may be a happy place to stay as long as the challenge remains." She could also become a consultant or put together her own group.

However, with whatever she does, she feels a commitment to make a contribution to education. She has, as she explained, "some sort of altruistic bent," to give back to society, part of what she feels she has taken.

She confessed, "I have been very lucky, being in the right place at the right time with the right skills." She believes she has made considerable impact with her work. However, she muses, "I sometimes wonder where I would have been had I been a man. Would I sit on the sixth floor of the Goddard Space Flight Center, in the director's office?"

NAOMI J. McAFEE

Electrical Engineering Manager

Naomi McAfee is a woman who enjoys meeting challenges. Throughout her childhood and her working career, she has been goaded onto greater heights by the excitement of accomplishing what others did not think was possible.

She is currently in charge of a $600 million budget and manages more than 250 professional engineers and fifty technical and support staff for the Westinghouse Defense and Electronics Systems Center, Design Assurance Systems and Research and Development Group.

Early Background and Education

Despite her impressive position, Naomi McAfee considers her entrance into engineering unlikely. She grew up on a farm as the fourth of five children. Studies have shown that women who enter engineering usually come from urban areas and are often the oldest child in their families. However, it is like McAfee to prove theories wrong and go her own way with a plan and a laugh.

From an early age she remembered being curious about how things worked. Her mother once warned her, "I am going out of the house. Do not take the piano apart." The piano did remain intact but Naomi McAfee took apart and reassembled other things.

She often helped her oldest brother, (who was also very supportive of her), with his tinkering. "I was his 'gopher,' bringing him tools and materials he needed, and in return, I learned many things I still use today, like tuning my car, or changing a tire.

"My parents were in favor of my getting all the education I could and having things easier than they did. Yet, my mom thought I was a little too competitive," she said.

"Phooey," she commented. "I never did buy that. Women have been taught that they are wrong if they use their capabilities to the utmost. I don't think this is wrong. I think this is the way a person should operate," she explained.

McAfee attended a small Kentucky school. Since she had more interest than any of the other students in technical problems, she was the one assigned to work on technical topics. She did a term paper on Madame Curie, whom she considered to be a brilliant woman and who was an inspiration. This paper and another one Naomi did on the atomic bomb greatly influenced her career.

After graduating from high school, she attended Western Kentucky State College where she first majored in chemistry. Half of the chemistry majors there were women, perhaps because the college had originally been a teachers' college. Later she changed to a major in physics, earning her bachelor's degree in that field. One professor told her, "I don't think a girl can make it in physics, but I'm willing to give you the chance." Again, she accepted the challenge and proved she could make it.

The physics classes were small—from four to twenty people. The small class size was an advantage," she recalls. We were more like a family than competing individuals. We all helped each other get through a set of experiments. The teacher knew how we were progressing without needing to test us.

She contrasted her experience in a small class with that of students she has visited at Purdue University and other colleges where engineering classes range between 300–400 students. Despite all the learning aides used in the large classes, McAfee said she would definitely opt for a small class. She suggested that women consider class size as well as other things when choosing an engineering school.

Employment Progression

Immediately after graduating from college in 1956, she was hired by Westinghouse to work on infrared research. However, by the time she arrived there, the contract she was to work on had been cancelled. She accepted another position with Westinghouse to do electrical engineering.

"Much of the math in physics and electrical engineering is similar. The major difference lies in the terminology." Because of this, she was able to make the change from physics to electrical engineering.

Like other young engineers, she began her work under the direction of a senior engineer. Her position first was assistant and then associate engineer. She and other engineers calculated mathematical models of projects to see how a product would work without actually building it. She also was responsible for monitoring subcontractor activities.

Four years later she was promoted to full engineer. She became the group leader responsible for the development of reliability prediction techniques. At this stage, she also was in charge of the design of experiments and system reliability analysis, reliability programs and vendor rating systems.

Two years later she held the rank of fellow engineer. Her responsibilities then included conducting and planning all technical studies pertaining to reliability, maintainability and availability of systems. She also directed the reliability program for the Special Airborne Missile Control System, the Radar Altimeter Reliability Enhancement Program and the Environmental Measurement Experiment for the Advanced Technology

Satellite Program. This included technical direction of five engineers, budget planning and administration.

As McAfee advanced in the corporation, so did her responsibility for the technical direction of others, budget planning, and administrative responsibilities. By this time, she was moving away from engineering per se into management.

Four years later she became a supervisory engineer. With this advance came responsibility for directing the reliability engineering efforts of all aerospace division and special programs. She supervised thirteen engineers and eleven clerks and technicians.

Two years later she was promoted to manager of reliability, maintainability and safety engineering. Her expanded responsibilities included direction of all engineering department reliability and maintainability. She also directed safety engineering and logistics planning activities in support of the Aerospace Division's development, equipment design and production programs. This included tripling her supervisory role. At this time she was in charge of forty-five engineers, as well as the budget planning, administration and capital equipment expenditures for the Failure Analysis Laboratory.

Her next promotion brought her the title of manager of quality and reliability engineering of the aerospace programs. Here she was in charge of planning, implementing and controlling all functions of reliability, quality maintainability and safety engineering. She had to develop concepts and new techniques for selection and training of personnel, as well as establish budgets, control expenditures, and maintain schedules. At this time she supervised seventy people, including two managers, three advisory engineers, three supervisory engineers and sixty-two other engineers.

Three years later her promotion to engineer, managing quality and reliability assurance doubled her reponsibilities. In this position she was in charge of planning, implementing, and managing all aspects of reliability, maintainability and safety engineering and quality assurance engineering for a large corporate group. She worked with military program personnel to sell and implement reliability programs on all defense and electronic systems product lines. Her department consisted of 158 people.

After twenty years with the Defense and Electronic Systems Center of Westinghouse in Baltimore, she spent a year commuting between Baltimore and corporate headquarters in Pittsburgh. She served as director of corporate strategic resources, and worked on the staff of the vice president for strategic resources. Her job was to look at what the corporation was doing and develop a five-year plan suggesting where the corporation should be going.

In addition, she helped the various divisions with their engineering problems. "The various business areas wrote plans that we critiqued and we could see how these fit into the total corporate structure," she explained. "This enabled us to see some of the problems that these divisions might be experiencing." This included reviewing and evaluating budgets submitted by various divisions, including defense, electronic components, elevator, heavy construction, meter, motor, and power system projects, process equipment and systems, switch gear, and transportation.

When she returned to Baltimore, she served for two years as executive assistant to the general manager of systems and technology divisions of the Defense and Electronic Systems Center. She assisted the general manager in managing and operating four divisions: aerospace, command and control, oceanic, and system development, with combined annual sales of more than $200 million a year.

She was responsible for technical problem solving on advanced electronic systems, profit planning, developing and implementing policy, long term, five year strategic planning, project managing, program scheduling, customer liaison, contract review, specification interpretation and implementation, engineering and production follow-through, design evaluation, human resource planning, and capital development.

Since 1979, she has been manager of design assurance and systems, and research and development divisions. She is responsible for planning, implementing and controlling all design assurance functions of development, design, integration, and testing of all programs under her jurisdiction.

Management

As a manager, she relies upon her professional background to support long-range planning and acquisition. She is interested in seeking good talent and planning and managing for the future. Some corporations employ financial experts as division heads. However, McAfee believes that only a person with a technical background can see the long-range implications of projects. "Decision-making by financial experts may be good up front, but down stream, it will kill you," she explained. However, she does rely on the advice of some top corporate financial advisers, as one element in her decision-making.

One of the things apparent in discussions with Naomi McAfee is her logical thought process. She sees what difficulty there is and then finds out what is needed to solve the problem. Then she lays out the various options to get the problem solved, examines what has to be done developmentally, fits the pieces together, and sees if the solution works. If it does, she runs with it.

Professional Associations

McAfee is active in several professional societies, including the American Society for Quality Control, the Society of Women Engineers, the Institute of Electrical and Electronic Engineers, the Reliability Society, the Federation of Organizations for Professional Women, the Engineers Joint Council, and the National Resource Council.

Advice to Women

Based on her own experience and from the vantage point of the professional associations to which she belongs, McAfee has some thoughts on engineering and women's role in it.

Communication. One of the keys to success in engineering is the ability to communicate. The engineer of today must be able to communicate, both orally and in writing, to describe what she is doing, so others may understand. While Albert Einstein was a recluse, he could write well and explain his ideas in written form.

You must be able to explain and communicate what you have to say to either a technical or political audience. This was just as true of Madame Curie and Lillian Gilbreth, one of the first systems engineers.

Goal Development. Another important aspect of a woman's professional growth is the development of goals for herself. These will need to be changed periodically. "When I get started in a new field, I revise my goals," says McAfee. "My goals now are very different from what they were last year. Too many people get hung up in seeing that they remain on track with their goals even though the situation has changed. A person must be flexible," she advised.

Many women in a corporation are not sure they should be where they are. This lack of self-confidence and inability to stand up for their rights harms women's chances for potential advancement. If women do not see themselves as having a rightful place in the corporation and then moving up in it, no one else will help them progress in their career either.

Discrimination. While Naomi McAfee is strongly pro-women, she believes that if a woman first thinks that the reason she did not get ahead was her sex, then she is probably trying to cop out.

"Yes," she admits, "In my own career I was discriminated against, but I liked what I did and the people with whom I did it. Now I have achieved a level where I can prevent a lot of discrimination from occurring.

"In the beginning a woman has a better advantage than a man because of equal employment opportunity and affirmative action," she states. "Once in a company, situations differ. No two companies handle a woman's rise in the corporation in the same way. However, with a company in a growth situation, you have a better chance of succeeding because you can get in on the ground floor and grow with the company, whereas in an older, more established area, the same growth potential is not possible because of the many layers of people above you," she concluded.

Overleaf: Sylvia Waller, shown in conference in her office in The Pentagon, is an aerospace engineer, a member of one of the smaller branches of engineering in the United States.

CHAPTER 8

AEROSPACE ENGINEERS

Aerospace engineering involves the design and solution of problems related to aircraft, rockets, satellites, and spacecraft. Problems may concern structure, stability, propulsion, control, analysis of vehicle operation, calculation of vehicle trajectories, and use of this knowledge for both aerospace and defense. Many aerospace engineers are employed in defense fields.

The Bureau of Labor Statistics said there were about 50,000 aerospace engineers employed in 1976, and an additional 1,500 are needed yearly. This makes aerospace engineering one of the smaller branches of engineering.

Employment of aerospace engineers is closely related to the level of federal expenditures on defense and space programs. When these are high, more aerospace engineers may be employed. When these are cut back, so are aerospace engineers. An aerospace engineer with a broad background of training and experience may more easily weather the problems of unemployment by switching fields.

In the fall of 1978, 520 women represented 6.5 percent of the 7,949 aerospace undergraduates enrolled in United States colleges and universities. That year, women represented only 2.9 percent of full-time graduate students enrolled in this field, according to *Engineering and Technology Enrollments, Fall, 1978,* prepared by the Engineering Manpower Commission.

Aerospace engineering is sometimes taught as part of mechanical engineering. However, it tends to be more scientific than older branches of engineering. Aerospace engineering depends heavily on mathematics and physics, especially the phenomena of fluid flow and structural designs of an analytic nature. Once an aerospace engineer makes a preliminary design, electronic and mechanical engineers usually carry out the detailed design. Aerospace engineering is closely related to metallurgical advances and advances in chemistry as well.

Related fields include submerged vessels (similar to aircraft), air cushion vehicles, ships, ground transportation systems, some phases of oceanography, and meteorology. Some people consider automotive and marine engineering, including naval architecture, to be related, specialized fields where similar concepts are applied.

Sylvia L. Waller, whose story is included here, plays a significant role in advising the Secretary of the Air Force on weapons systems. She herself has a broad base in electrical engineering and might also have been included in the section on electrical engineering, except that her current work involves many special aerospace problems.

SYLVIA L. WALLER

Air Force Adviser

Sylvia Waller radiates energy, whether she is striding down the halls of the Pentagon or simply sitting in her office discussing electrical engineering. She has a quick mind which enjoys challenges, and she is self-confident enough to handle them.

Waller is scientific and technical advisor to the Assistant Chief of Staff of the U.S. Air Force for Studies and Analysis. She is special advisor on weapon systems testing, evaluation, survivability, and electronic warfare.

Sylvia Waller has several 'firsts' to her credit. She was the first person to earn an electrical engineering degree from Brooklyn Polytechnic Institute. She was the first woman member in the electrical engineering department at the Massachusetts Institute of Technology. In addition, she was the first woman to hold a supergrade position in the Air Force. Now she is one of the first women in the Senior Executive Service attached to the Air Force.

In her present position, she supervises and coordinates testing and evaluation of strategic large weapon systems. To do this, she examines the specifications for these weapon systems before they are developed, both for their cost and effectiveness under simulated battle conditions.

Early Background and Education

Despite her accomplishments, her entrance into engineering was unusual. "There was no one in my family who was an engineer," Waller explains. "My older sister became an elementary school teacher. My interest in engineering was self-generated. I felt like a pioneer. I wanted to be different. It kept me moving.

"Even in elementary school I was innovative among my girl friends. I volunteered to go into woodworking class, then only open to boys. At the earliest opportunity to be different, I chose to be.

"When I was in high school, I remember ordering a crystal radio set. Then I wired the house with the antenna, and my family was horrified for fear that I would electrocute them all," she recalled with a laugh.

"However, my parents were very supportive. They wanted me to do whatever I wanted to do and encouraged me, especially since I did well.

"When I went to college, I was not certain whether I should go into English, Latin or math because I always wanted to write." Ironically, now much of Waller's writing is classified and can only be read by a limited audience. Yet, "math was such a cinch for me, I majored in it," she said.

Waller earned her bachelor's degree in mathematics, cum laude, from Adelphi University, then an all women's college, now coed. During the evening, the school offered engineering courses "which I found fascinating and saw clearly that engineering was my field.

Career Progression

"When I graduated with my math degree, two years of engineering, and draft exempt, I found that many engineering companies were eager for my services. One of my senior math professors had worked for Bell Telephone Labs and considered it one of the finest engineering labs in the world, so I accepted a position there," she said.

At Bell Telephone Labs she was a junior electrical engineer and technical writer. She continued to take engineering courses at night.

She left Bell Telephone Labs to get her master's degree. "I recognized that I needed my master's degree to get ahead," she said. "I waited till the War (World War II) was over and the Massachusetts Institute of Technology (MIT) offered me a staff position." She served on the electrical engineering research staff at MIT while she was working on her master's degree.

She met her husband at MIT where he was stationed as a military engineer. "Where we went for the first twenty years of marriage depended on where he was stationed," she explained.

"I had a comfortable feeling that with my engineering background and breadth of experience, you could drop me anywhere and I would find an interesting job. It was probably my good fortune that I was forced to move so often," she said.

"Job changing in engineering is the norm for advancement. People who stay in one job early in their careers for a long period of time are sometimes thought to be incapable of advancement," she explained.

"Engineering, and especially electrical engineering, is so broadly-based in the physical sciences that you have an unlimited horizon of different things you can be doing within the field. Being an electrical engineer gives you the option to do almost anything your professional interests dictate," she explained.

For Waller, this has meant working for three branches of the Department of Defense: Army, Navy, and Air Force. Early in her career she was producing technical filmstrips for Air Force training programs. She prepared a complete series of these films on operation, maintenance, and installation of new ground radar equipment and on joint Army-Air Force operations in a combat area.

Prior to this, she worked for the Army Signal Corps Board at Fort Monmouth, NJ. She served as a technical writer and an advisor on new equipment and procedures for the operational use of Signal Corps equipment.

In 1953, she served with the U.S. Navy Bureau of Ordnance as an engineer in the fire-control radar system. Here she was responsible for supervising production, installation, and maintenance of fire control radar programs for shipboard use. She also analyzed new construction and ongoing fleet programs to determine their radar equipment needs.

After this, Waller became the technical director of the Missile Countermeasures Laboratory for the U.S. Air Force Missile Test Center at Holloman Air Force Base in New Mexico. Here she was responsible for testing and evaluating the susceptibility of air-to-air and air-to-ground missiles to enemy countermeasures.

For three years thereafter, she served as a senior technical advisor and consultant on electronics systems for the Army Aviation Board in Fort Rucker, AL. She also represented this board at conferences on aviation, electronics, and surveillance equipment.

From this position she went to the Institute for Defense Analysis in Arlington, VA, as a senior staff member. Here for seventeen years, she directed studies involving operational evaluations and designs of large-scale joint service tests for air-to-ground, air-to-air, and electronic warfare systems for the Secretary of Defense. She also participated in studies of strategic and tactical offensive and defensive systems.

She had expected to remain indefinitely at this position, but the Air Force asked her to become a scientific and technical advisor to the Assistant Chief of Staff and she did.

When asked about the various changes in her professional life, she replied, "I let it flow and take advantage of every opportunity that comes my way. I am a great believer that if doors do not upon up, you can go around and look for another open door," Sylvia Waller said. She attributes much of her success to chance and the things that did *not* happen.

For example, she did not enter the Women's Army Corps (WACS) because they refused to give her the same rank the Army would have given an equivalently educated man. "Thereafter came an even more challenging professional opportunity," she said.

However, she added, she has had no problems with professional barriers because she is a woman. "From my earliest days at Bell Labs, men have always been tremendously supportive and enthusiastic and have been so surprised that here is a woman interested in this usually male field. My interest in engineering has given men engineers a sense of satisfaction to sponsor a woman who is apparently qualified.

"At the Army Aviation Board at Fort Rucker, I was more qualified than some of the men, and fought to get higher job-grade levels for myself and the men. I was pulling them up and helping them, so they did not object. This was also true in the Air Force and Navy positions," she explained.

Looking up from her desk in her Pentagon office, Sylvia Waller, commented on the role of the engineer. "The engineer is part of an organization within the structure of management, and yet at a level of the practical design work. The engineer, in contrast to the research scientist, works for someone else or the organization, not for her or himself. Science is different with its emphasis on individual research.

"In engineering, each development is a continuum built on the last. This makes it difficult to break into engineering from a non-engineering field," she explained.

Yet, Waller commented, "There are many women who call themselves 'engineers.' In some organizations, I saw women come into entry level jobs without going through the engineering school route. They then tried engineering jobs and complained that they were not being given the opportunities. But I believe they were not as qualified as they could have been to take on increasingly difficult work. They had reached their limits.

"A person who enters engineering from another field has not had training in systems analysis thinking. This is necessary for engineering work," she said.

"Engineering is a difficult course at whatever school one chooses. It requires tremendous out-of-classroom work and commitment. Few women were willing to apply that much dedicated effort in their college years. Engineering requires early and lasting dedication. Otherwise, you will not make it," she warned.

"Today there is a lack of truly qualified women in engineering. It is hard to jump in and be competitive unless you are equal to men by virtue of your education and professional training and experience. My degrees, schools and the places I have worked have always made me competitive with men. Without the support of men I would have been held back. I have never sensed that being a woman was a disqualifier," she said.

Professional Associations

Another important area for the engineer is in professional associations. They "give you exposure to others who you would not normally meet in the course of your own work," Ms. Waller said. "This exposure establishes a set of contacts, so when something comes up, the people who met you may call upon you. This puts you in line for further professional opportunities."

Waller is quite concerned that only a few women are involved in professional association activities. The professional engineering societies encourage participation of members, but do not specifically seek women. Women are not accustomed to being the aggressor and often wait to be asked. Waller believes this is a mistake.

"Men see that participation in a professional association is helpful to their professional image and professional advancement. Women in engineering must learn this lesson," Waller said.

She is active in professional societies, especially the Institute of Electrical and Electronic Engineers, Inc. (IEEE) and the Military Operations Research Society (MORS).

While she was active in the Society of Women Engineers (SWE) in the 1950s, she has not been active there in the last twenty years. "Women can serve themselves best by being active and vocal in general professional societies and not in special women's societies," she says. "Getting the best visibility can be most helpful to women coming along in their professional fields."

Waller also participated extensively in scientific advisory groups. In 1977 she was a technical advisor to the Strategic Penetration Technology group. She now serves on the Scientific Advisory Group on Tactical Aircraft Survivability Joint Test and Evaluation, as well as on the Joint Cruise Missile Survivability Advisory Panel. She also participates in the Air Force Cruise Missile Survivability Steering Group, and several other technical advisory groups, including one for the Advanced Research Projects Agency of the Department of Defense.

In addition, Waller has worked for the Massachusetts Institute of Technology's Educational Council and their alumnae club. "I interviewed many women interested in MIT and tried to encourage them to enter engineering rather than go the math or science route," she said.

Family Life

On top of all this activity, Waller has raised two children. She said she never took extensive time off after they were born. "I continued to work when I had my children. That came about because I was a professional before I was married. There was no question of my continuing to work. I found live-in housekeepers to watch our two daughters. I was fortunate in finding very competent persons. Without full-time help, I don't think women can serve a dual role.

"I recently asked my daughters, now both in their 30s, if they felt cheated because I worked. They replied they never felt this way. In part, this came about by having very good household help. When I came home, I could devote myself to the children rather than the housework. Except for the workday, I was free to be with them. I did not have to worry about making meals or doing the wash.

"I think it would be difficult to take time off to spend solely with the children and remain competitive with the men in the workforce. If you did take years off, upon your return you would have to drop back a notch or two, losing the flow and progress in your career. In any profession there is an 'age-experience salary curve.' If a woman takes years off, and then goes back, her lower level of experience at her advancing age works against her," Waller explained.

Sylvia Waller regrets that neither of her daughters is interested in engineering, because she believes there are many excellent opportunities in the field for women who are willing to dedicate themselves to getting a quality engineering education and then to devoting the requisite time and energy to their careers.

Overleaf: Dr. Thelma Estrin, biomedical engineer, works in a professional specialty which has existed for only about a third of a century. (Photo: Courtesy Al Hicks, UCLA School of Medicine)

CHAPTER 9

BIOMEDICAL ENGINEERING

Biomedical engineering is the application of engineering principles and concepts to living systems. The field is about thirty years old. The relative newness and growth in this area mean that ideas and people in it are not as entrenched as in other engineering disciplines. This allows women greater opportunity for advancement, according to Dr. Thelma Estrin, whose story follows.

Because of the opportunities in this field and perhaps due to their traditional interest in life sciences, more women are enrolled in biomedical engineering than in any other engineering curriculum. Of the 2,654 undergraduates in this field in the fall of 1978, almost a quarter (647) were women, according to *Engineering & Technology Enrollments, Fall, 1978,* prepared by the Engineering Manpower Commission. Of the 700 graduate students in this field in 1978, women represented more than 13 percent of those enrolled.

Biomedical engineers generally may be classified into three major types: research, design and development, and clinical engineers.

The research engineer is employed by a university or research institute as a research scientist. In 1975, there were approximately 2,000 of these individuals employed. Most held Ph.D's. In their research to develop a prototype, they use sophisticated instrumentation to make experimental observations through the use of advanced mathematical techniques for analyzing data. They use computers to model and simulate biological systems and to better understand fundamental biological mechanisms.

Typical of the research they perform is basic research into the physical properties of biological matter and its interface with living tissue; pattern recognition of electrical signals generated by the heart, muscle and brain; studies of human regulating and control systems at organ and cellular levels; radiation treatment planning; image processing; diagnostic radiology and modeling and simulation of cardiovascular, respiratory, excretory, gastrointestinal, or endocrine systems.

One of the newer areas is neuroscience. This interdisciplinary area is concerned with behavior in relation to the brain.

The second type of biomedical engineer, the design and development engineer, takes the prototype developed by the research engineer and turns it into a usable product. This includes the design and building of diagnostic, therapeutic, and prosthetic devices. In 1975, there were some 3,000 of these design and development engineers. The potential for future job opportunities in this area is also very good.

Diagnostic equipment is continually redesigned and improved. A biomedical engineer might design instrumentation for medical imaging, in which a diagnosis is made through noninvasive techniques such as x-ray, ultrasound, or nuclear imaging. Other areas include microelectronic recording and display systems for patient monitoring of biological signals, and internal-structure imagers using x-ray, radioactive tracers, and ultrasonic devices.

Therapeutic devices include heart-lung machines, home dialysis units, respirators, defibrillators, simulators, and radiation therapy machines. Examples of prosthetic devices are artificial limbs, pacemakers, heart valves, hip joints, artificial kidneys, and sensors and aids for the blind and deaf.

The third area is clinical engineering. This is where the greatest growth is occurring, according to Dr. Estrin. The clinical engineer in a hospital is becoming an established part of the clinical team.

In 1975, there were about 3,000 engineers in this category employed by larger hospitals. Most of them held either a bachelor's degree or a master's degree. They assist medical center personnel in problem definition, equipment specification and bid evaluation, and construction and design of special purpose electronic equipment not commercially available. They may also be responsible for developing methods of calibrating and performance-checking of instrumentation, establishing and supervising standards and safety, and managing life-support systems. Clinical engineers may also have responsibility for application of computers and automation to handle information in clinical chemistry laboratories, intensive care units, surgical recovery suites, and EKG laboratories. Computers are used to generate laboratory reports, schedule and bill patients, control inventories, and establish data banks for research and preventive health studies. Increasingly, computers are being used to record patient records.

Training for these three roles in biomedical engineering differs. The research engineer needs a strong mathematical background and probably a Ph.D. The developmental engineer needs a strong design background. The clinical engineer needs at least a bachelor's degree with additional course work in computer science and psychology.

Today, more than 200 universities and engineering schools in the United States offer courses in biomedical engineering. There are three routes into this field.

The first is to attend an engineering school in a traditional program such as electrical, mechanical, or chemical engineering, adding courses in biomedical engineering later. A person could get additional exposure by choosing topics from biomedical areas for any research reports or projects.

The second route one may take is to enroll in an interdisciplinary program. Here you would be trained in one of the classical branches of engineering but would also take some formally prescribed courses in life sciences. Typically, a biomedical engineer trained in this way becomes a member of a team that includes people from the life sciences.

The third approach is through a program in which biomedical engineering is offered as a separate discipline. This may include a clinical engineering internship as a part of the curriculum.

In one clinically oriented program, students in the biomedical engineering classes are assigned to work with specific patients in a hospital.

In discussion with the patients, and supervised by medical personnel, they analyze the patient's problems and design cosmetic or rehabilitative devices for the patient's use. Students with such a background have very good training for clinical engineering positions in hospitals. A clinical certification of competency program is also available which may enhance prestige and job-getting potential.

THELMA ESTRIN

Bio-Engineer

Dr. Thelma Estrin is a pioneer in the growing field of bio-engineering. She has done much to popularize the field, as well as expand its horizons. In addition, she has taught and directed many of its current practitioners.

Dr. Estrin was among the first to apply computer techniques to analyze the electrical activity of the nervous system. Initially interested in the use of computers in brain research, her interests now are in the area of computer technology for medicine. She believes that in ten to twenty years all medical transactions will be electronically recorded.

Dr. Estrin believes that her story may be useful to women contemplating an engineering career because she presents two models: one as a woman demonstrating outstanding success and the other as a woman who has never gotten tenure at a university.

She muses about her entrance into this field. At one time she could not get a job in electrical engineering either as a teacher or a practitioner, but there was a job open in the bio-engineering field and she accepted that. This unexpected turn of events led her into further research and she became excited about the field of bio-engineering.

Early Experiences and Training

Dr. Estrin grew up in New York. By the time she had completed high school, World War II had begun. Women were encouraged to take over the jobs left by men who went into military service or defense-related work. She took a three-months course at Steven's Institute to become an engineering assistant.

She enjoyed the work and decided that engineering was indeed for her. She went to engineering school, with her husband, at the University of Wisconsin, Madison, where they both earned their bachelor's, master's and doctoral degrees in electrical engineering.

During her training Dr. Estrin learned about the behavior of electrical fields on the surface of the head, principles now used in electroencephalograms and brain research. She thought it would be exciting to study this more.

In the 1950s, when she was finished with her schooling, "Times were different," she explained. She accompanied her husband when he went to the prestigious Institute for Advanced Study at Princeton University to be a member of the team building one of the first electronic computers.

When she arrived at Princeton, she interviewed with RCA, the only large employer of engineers in that area. They appreciated her credentials, but among reasons they gave for not hiring her, was a lack of bathroom facilities for women professionals. She insists, however, this was just an excuse for not hiring a woman.

Through friends who worked at Columbia University, "I got a job at the Neurological Institute there. This was a fortuitous turn," she reflected.

"If I had gotten a job at either Princeton or RCA, I might not be where I am today. I might not have gone into bioengineering, though I already knew it was a fascinating area."

At the Neurology Department, she conducted research on the electrical activity of the nervous system. She also had engineering responsibility for the instrumentation in the EEG (electroencephalogram) laboratory of Columbia Presbyterian Neurological Institute.

While her husband was at the Institute for Advanced Studies at Princeton, he was invited to Israel to build the first computer. Dr. Estrin accompanied him. In 1954, she became a member of the Electronic Computer Group at the Weizmann Institute of Science in Israel.

They returned to America where her husband accepted a position at the University of California, Los Angeles (UCLA). He is currently chairman of the UCLA Computer Department. Dr. Thelma Estrin could not join the faculty at that time because of a nepotism rule which did not allow a husband and wife to be on the same faculty. This rule is no longer operative at UCLA.

During this period, Dr. Thelma Estrin taught junior college and did private consulting. Later she obtained an appointment to the Brain Research Institute of the UCLA Medical School. Here she led in the development of one of the first integrated computer-based laboratories for neuro-scientists. This facility evolved into the Institute's Data Processing laboratory, of which she was appointed director in 1970.

"Things were good here when research money was plentiful, but when it dried up, there were problems," she said.

In about 1973-74, the women's movement began to jolt her consciousness. She looked around her and wondered why she did not have tenure. "However," she reflected, "neither then nor now has UCLA made a great effort to promote women to tenured positions, although the prestigious Massachusetts Institute of Technology has long done so."

Awards

Throughout her career Dr. Estrin has received many national honors. In 1975, she received the Distinguished Service Citation from the University of Wisconsin as an electrical engineer whose technical competence and research direction have produced important advances in the application of computers to bio-medical needs.

In 1977, she was the fifth woman named a Fellow of the Institute for Electrical and Electronics Engineers, for her contribution to design and application of computer systems for neuro-physiological and brain research.

In 1979, she received an outstanding engineer merit award for contributions to bio-medical engineering from the Institute for Advanced Study of the University of Southern California.

Despite these national honors, Dr. Estrin is still an adjunct professor and not a full or tenured professor. She teaches the use of computers and electronics for medicine. She is a certified clinical engineer and once practiced in this area though she does not now. She is currently particularly interested in the application of computer technology to the whole field of medical records.

As an adjunct professor, she has not had graduate students to advise. Graduate students are a continual source of renewal and provide a way for professionals to work out their ideas, write, and publish their findings. Such publications help a person advance in the academic community, she explained.

She speaks frankly about the discrimination she has faced and admitted that today she probably would have been a dean or head of an institute had she been a man with similar qualifications. Since she was not a part of the permanent faculty, she was excluded from the many departmental meetings and other informal contacts that help a person establish credibility with peers. Not being seen, she was passed over for many excellent positions. She also believes that leadership subconsciously seeks men for high positions and does not consider that women can be managers or directors of large, powerful technological organizations.

Professional Associations

Outside of the university, Dr. Estrin is widely known and respected. She has made a national career for herself through membership in several professional associations. Besides being a Fellow of IEEE and very active in it, she was formerly head of the IEEE Professional Opportunities for Women Committee. She has been president of IEEE's Biomedical Engineering Society and vice president of Publications for IEEE. In 1973 she ran for an IEEE elected office and won by a large plurality of votes. "Now I am on the board of directors of IEEE. I feel that they realized they needed a woman," Dr. Estrin explained.

She has also served as vice president of the Alliance for Engineering in Medicine and Biology. She is United States member of the International Federation of Medical and Biological Engineers.

She is also a member of the American Electroencephalographic Society, the Society for Neuroscience, the American Association for the Advancement of Science, the Association for Women in Mathematics, Sigma Xi, and Tau Beta Pi.

Commenting on her membership in the Society of Women Engineers, Dr. Estrin said, "It is quite thrilling to attend their conferences and see hundreds of professional women. The Society of Women Engineers has not always been very strong on women's rights, though it recently did support the Equal Rights Amendment (ERA). Now it functions as a support group through which women help each other with career planning, which is quite important," she said. However, Dr. Estrin predicts that in ten years this group will self-destruct because it will no longer be needed, and women will receive their support from other areas.

For example, she notes that support groups in major industries are becoming more common. At the Aerospace Corporation, where she sits on the board of trustees, a woman's committee functions as a support group. Dr. Estrin admits that a woman serving on the board of any industry is rare. Selection to board membership indicates great professional acceptance of the woman.

Dr. Estrin explained the importance of membership in professional associations. "Professional associations can be very helpful. It's like rehearsing in the wings. It is an opportunity to interact with men. You can feel your way and not be threatened as you would be in your job. In a professional association you can learn a lot and make a lot of contacts. The professional associations enable you to do very interesting things both managerially and technically. I have put on conferences, organized sessions and kept technically aware."

The two major technical associations for people in computing are the IEEE Computer Society and the Association for Computing Machinery. "The latter attracts more math teachers, so it has more women in it," Dr. Estrin explained. In 1979, an association for women in computing was formed and Dr. Estrin is a member of its board of directors. Its purpose is to encourage communication among women in all areas of the information processing field.

"Interestingly," she says, "many of the active people in professional societies tend not to be of U.S. origin. They are very concerned about their professional advancement and they value our system," she said. "The current generation tends not to become active in professional associations because so many things are competing for their attention. Because there are lots of jobs open now, they don't realize how professional associations can advance their careers."

Dr. Estrin belongs to professional associations because "I am concerned with the transmission and social implications of technology, engineering education, and the promotion of women," she explained.

Personal Life

In addition to her work, Dr. Estrin is the mother of three daughters who are also pursuing professional careers. Her eldest daughter is a physician. Her second daughter has a master's degree in electrical engineering and computer science and is an engineer manager at a large company. The youngest is getting her electrical engineering degree at Berkeley and is president of the Women in Computer Science and Engineering. She plans to enter public policy and technology.

Dr. Estrin admitted that she has little time for other hobbies or interests.

Advice to Women

Dr. Estrin firmly believes that engineering for women is an excellent career choice. Engineering offers women a wide spectrum of activities from which to choose. A woman can enter engineering as a technician, or enter at the next level with a B.S. in electro-technology. This degree is awarded to people who desire a simpler, less analytical, and more practical application of engineering.

Dr. Estrin suggests that if a woman has a choice between science and engineering, she has a better chance of success in engineering. "To make it as a scientist," she said, "requires study at the Ph.D level. Then if you are lucky, you may be the one chosen to join the faculty of a prestigious institution. However, since there are so few jobs and a declining college-age population, the competition is quite fierce. Only the most brilliant make it." By contrast, there are fourteen jobs for each student with a B.S. in computer science or electrical engineering with experience in computer science.

To become an electrical engineer or enter another professional field of engineering, Dr. Estrin believes a woman should be at least a B math student in order to succeed. "If a woman can handle the math, electrical engineering is an exceptional career choice, especially in the computer field," she emphasized.

"Women should also consider careers in engineering management. There are lots of jobs for women here. However, a woman should prepare herself with at least two years of experience before entering management. Women make excellent managers because they tend to be more interpersonal, more sensitive to people's feelings, and better organized. However, they do need a sound technical foundation in order to direct the people under them.

In electrical engineering, as in many engineering fields, discoveries and technological advances occur rapidly. If a person is in management, she does not have to keep up with the technology quite as much as those in research or those on-the-line. Her job is to plan, direct, and make decisions.

"Today, there are few women managers. However, this is beginning to change. Women can rise if they are willing to devote the time, energy and devotion to the job.

"However, a woman who is interested in only a 9-to-5 position may be able to find this in engineering, also. There are many levels of engineering. They offer a woman many ways she can go," Dr. Estrin said.

CHAPTER 10

CHEMICAL ENGINEERING

In 1976, there were 50,000 chemical engineers employed in the United States. Each year an additional 2,100 openings are expected for chemical engineers, according to the Bureau of Labor Statistics.

In the fall of 1978, 5,800 women comprised 19.4 percent of the total 29,844 students in chemical engineering enrolled in United States colleges and universities. In 1978, women made up 9.1 percent of the total 3,687 graduate students enrolled full-time in chemical engineering, according to *Engineering and Technology Enrollments, Fall, 1978,* prepared by the Engineering Manpower Commission.

Chemical engineering deals with the design, analysis, management, and control of industrial and other operations involving chemical processes. Because of the complexity involved, chemical engineers usually specialize in a particular operation or area.

Some chemical engineers design equipment and chemical plants and determine methods for manufacturing a product.

Chemical engineers generally begin with the basic scientific data on chemical reactions observed by research chemists. In the laboratory, the chemical engineer develops engineering data for the various steps in the process of changing the starting material into a product. The chemical engineer attempts to find new applications of laboratory discoveries.

By studying manufacturing problems, the chemical engineer may develop new chemical processes. These processes may be used in the development of adhesives, nuclear materials, fermentation, or many other areas. In these operations, economic   evaluations are quite important.

Chemical engineers may work with a variety of products: petroleum, synthetic products, corroding materials, or such items as textiles, papers, detergents, insecticides, drugs, or plastics.

Janet Embrey, whose story appears in this chapter, works on thermal battery projects. Based on her chemistry background, she was able to cut costs and improve the finished product for several projects.

Dr. Maryly Van Leer Peck, whose story is also in this section, is currently teaching a class in chemical engineering. The variety of things she has been able to do in her career provides an inspiring example to other chemical engineers.

MARYLY VAN LEER PECK

Chemical Engineer

Diversity seems to be one of the hallmarks of the career of Maryly Van Leer Peck. "I have been involved in small and big universities, industry and government. I have many options, but I like education. This is where I believe my greatest interests and talents lie. My greatest talent is dealing with people. I enjoy a reputation for being a very good teacher," she commented.

Dr. Peck has twenty-eight years experience as a chemical engineer and educator. In between industrial and government jobs, she was dean of a college in Guam. There she taught undergraduate students everything from science, to math, to engineering. She is currently dean of undergraduate curriculum for the University of Maryland, University College.

In 1979, Dr. Peck served as a consultant to Urban Pathfinders, Inc., an engineering consulting firm. In this role, she participated in the Amtrak Commuter Conflict study to analyze the effective use of the railway in the Northeast Corridor by both Amtrak and commuter trains.

The men working with her were impressed with her ability to assimilate information on railroading. She believes her training in engineering taught her to think logically and systematically, to grasp the problems involved in a project and find intelligent solutions.

She believes that with an engineering background you can do anything if you put your mind to it. "Engineers have logical minds and use systematic approaches. They can consume a great deal of information and sort things out logically," she explained.

Early Influences

Dr. Peck's interest in engineering stemmed from her home environment. Her father was an engineering educator and her mother was both an architect and an artist. Dr. Peck attended high school in Atlanta, Georgia where her father was president of Georgia Tech.

After high school she spent a year at Duke University and then transferred to Vanderbilt University. In 1951, she received her bachelor's degree in chemical engineering, *magna cum laude,* and married five days laters.

Career Progression

Her first job was as a chemical engineer at the Naval Research Lab in Washington, D.C. Here she did research on solid fuels.

A year later, during the Korean War, she worked at Camp LeJeune's Medical Field Research Lab doing work in camouflage and other chemical engineering projects. When she became pregnant she was required to quit, even though, as she said, "It was obvious that I could and would continue to work."

After her husband's stint in the Marines, the family moved to Florida and she earned her master's degree in chemical engineering. Her thesis was on "Heat Transfer to Clouds of Particles of Various Concentrations of Elevated Temperatures." While working on her degree she was first a graduate assistant, then an associate in research and finally an instructor at the school.

Three years later the family moved to Georgia. She worked at the Georgia Tech Experiment Station as a chemical engineer in the product-testing branch. "Companies throughout the South asked us to test their products and analyze their systems for making their product environmentally sound. This involved a lot of different kinds of testing of systems, including gas analysis and pollution," Dr. Peck explained. She also taught part-time as a lecturer at Georgia State College.

In 1959, she received a National Science Foundation Fellowship and returned to the University of Florida to work on her Ph.D. Her doctoral dissertation was on "The Effect of Chemical Reaction on Absorption Rates in Laminar and Resident Zones." For this she developed a mathematical model for the mass transfer occurring in packed absorption towers used to clean fluids and gases.

She explained why more school was necessary; "I wanted to continue in education, and the doctorate is the necessary ticket in higher education," she said.

After her graduate work she went to California to work for Rocketdyne, North American Aviation. She was a senior research engineer working in the field of hybrid fuels. "Though I was part of a group, I tested my own ideas. Occasionally others made suggestions or I helped them," she said.

After two years there, she spent six months traveling across the country lecturing about "Women in Engineering." During this time she supported herself and her family by the honorariums she received from her lectures. Since her husband was in theology school at this time, she had to make provisions for her family, which now included four children.

When her husband finished up his work at the seminary, he was assigned to a church in North Carolina. Dr. Peck managed to get a job at a nearby college, first as an associate and then as a full professor of mathematics.

In 1966, her husband was appointed Vicar of Guam and his reponsibilities with the Episcopal Church included St. John's Episcopal School in Guam. For three years she was academic director of St. John's Episcopal School. After a year and a half she was asked to be chairman and professor of physical sciences at the University of Guam.

"I have as much math as engineering, so I agreed to head up the physical sciences division at the University of Guam. For the next year and a half, I held two full-time jobs. I was the only chairman of any division with a full teaching load. However, that was really because I enjoy teaching," she emphasized. In 1973, she was appointed dean of the College of Business and Applied Technology at the University of Guam.

Currently, she is in a similar position at the University of Maryland. "The reason I am in education is that I enjoy both young adults and older adults," she said. "I teach a whole gamut of people now, and it's fun. I have traditional students (18 to 20-year-olds) full time when I am teaching chemical engineering for the College Park Campus."

In reflecting on her career, Dr. Peck concludes, "I didn't have some of the difficulties of some women. I did well in school, and therefore I had a good academic background and had proved myself. There may have been some personality problems I encountered but I don't feel there was gross discrimination.

"I have gone back to work in industry several times to prove that I could. Most women of my vintage who have succeeded had to be very positive about what they wanted to do. I have very definite ideas and high standards for myself, and I understand that my children feel they have high standards to live up to.

"I don't want to be selected for a job because I am a woman. As a professional I would like to think I was selected because I was very good.

"Yet, I want women to have opportunities. I want to open doors for them. Right now engineering is one of the better professions because with a technical background you can do so many things.

"If a woman wants to enter engineering, the field is open. A young woman has be sure her talents lie in this area. Then she must be academically prepared in high school to handle the engineering curriculum in college. Not everybody has the kind of talent it takes to be an engineer," she concluded.

JANET MARIE EMBREY

Project Engineer, Thermal Batteries

Janet Embrey provides an example of a woman who entered engineering without formal training in engineering. Although her entrance was through the sciences, she admitted, "Formal studies may be required as my career progresses, depending on the path chosen." She also noted, "I would find it difficult to obtain an engineering position in another field without a formal degree."

Embrey earned her Bachelor of Science degree in chemistry from Towson State University in Towson, Maryland in 1976.

Until recently she served as a project engineer at Catalyst Research Corporation, a subsidiary of Mine Safety Appliances, in Baltimore, Maryland. She is now employed in a similar capacity at another firm.

Her job at Catalyst Research Corporation required a knowledge of several disciplines: chemistry, mechanical engineering, industrial engineering, and thermodynamics. "With the exception of the chemical background, knowledge of other disciplines has been gained through experience and self-study," she explained. "It is not as uncommon as it seems for a chemist to have this type of position."

Embrey continued, "While my career path has deviated from my fellow classmates who are working in quality control or research labs, and my starting salary was substantially below the average for graduating chemists, I felt that the long-term aspects and opportunities outweighed the initial discrepancy. This has proven to be true.

"As a project engineer, my position involved the manufacturing of thermal batteries to meet military specifications. This work was done on a project basis for each contract and required coordination of efforts of all departments through all phases of the project. Each design was unique and required the direct participation of the project engineer in all areas, including working with customers. Some areas of direct involvement included: initial feasibility analysis and proposal, cost study, and bid preparation. Other aspects of this job included component selection, prototype evaluation and assembly techniques, and tool and fixture set-ups. It also involved process instruction documentation, production methods analysis, and direction and scheduling."

To get a better idea of what this meant, she described five projects she directed. "In one project, more than 25,000 units were produced under my direction, while maintaining high product quality and keeping losses to a minimum. The emphasis here was on reducing costs by improving production procedures, material flow, and scheduling. Continual monitoring of battery performance with respect to assembly and component variables was employed.

"In another project, I designed parts and selected assembly methods unique for this small-size battery. I was proud of this project because normal turnaround time for a project of this type is seven to eight months, and we accomplished our goal in four.

"Another project I directed was given to me because of my good record. It had previously experienced high costs. Under my direction, production was increased from 50 to 300 units daily. I did this by instituting advanced assembly techniques. I helped increase yield by 10 percent by modification of the design. All together, 5,000 units were produced without a single lot failure. The occurrence of voltage noise during discharge was drastically reduced through tighter control of assembly methods.

"I also worked on one experimental project to study process control, processing, and variables contributing to batch-to-batch variations of raw materials. In this project, we also studied the effects on battery performance.

"I was put in charge of another contract for thermal batteries that had previously had poor-to-marginal battery discharge performance. The particular battery I worked on was unique in that it had a long-life and required a medium current drain. I conducted and arranged component variables in a matrix study. I helped thermally balance the battery to an optimum operating temperature. Then I identified the battery component variables so that maximum discharge performance and life was obtained. As a result, twenty lots of fifty units each were subsequently produced without a single lot failure."

Sexual Discrimination

About sexual discrimination, Embrey noted: "I have found some prefer- ence for males over females and the need to prove myself, specifically in matters dealing with mechanical operations and tooling design. For instance, sometimes there is resistance to accepting my technical sugges- tions for improvements or designs until such suggestions are supported by male coworkers.

"I feel that a woman pursuing an engineering career has far greater difficulty than a woman following a nonscientific path into business. I have found salaries for women lower than their male counterparts, although this is not always the case.

"Also I believe there is still some reluctance to hire a woman over a man in engineering, which I haven't observed in other scientific disci- plines such as chemistry or biology," Embrey said.

"I feel there is a need for informing women who are interested in an engineering career as to what to expect on the job. They should know what kinds of obstacles they may encounter and be prepared to make a real commitment to their careers. Rewards will be forthcoming," she stated.

Embrey, who is single, commented, "I would sincerely respect any woman who could combine the two roles of mother and professional engineer during the initial phase of her career because the demands required from the job are high. I personally would find great difficulty raising a family until I was well established in my career."

CHAPTER 11

CIVIL AND STRUCTURAL ENGINEERING

According to the Bureau of Labor Statistics, in 1976, there were 155,000 civil engineers employed in this country. Each year 8,900 more are needed.

In the fall of 1978, 4,584 women composed 10.4 percent of the 44,162 undergraduates enrolled in civil engineering in the United States colleges and universities. In graduate studies, the 429 women composed 7.4 percent of the 5,807 enrolled in civil engineering, according to *Engineering and Technology Enrollments, Fall, 1978,* prepared by the Engineering Manpower Commission.

Most civil engineers work for government agencies. Many work for consulting engineering and architectural firms.

KATHRYN E. ANNER

Structural Engineer

Kathryn Anner, a structural engineer at Weidlinger Associates, New York, described the role of a structural engineer to a conference on women in engineering. "As a structural engineer, I am a graduate civil engineer specializing in the structural design of buildings and bridges rather than the design of roads, dams or sewers. In school you receive training in all of these specialties, in addition to getting fundamental courses in electrical and mechanical engineering," Anner explained.

The civil engineer may also be responsible for the conception, design, construction, or management of transportation, water resources or urban development. He or she may specialize in city planning, foundation engineering, sanitation, environmental engineering or architectural engineering.

"The job of structural engineers is to make the building stand up," Anner explained. "They also have an obligation to the owner to design the building as economically as possible, to the architect to help make it as aesthetically pleasing as possible, and to the contractor to make it as easy to build as possible.

"As you can gather from this, the engineer's job is not just one of designing beams and columns. It encompasses a great deal more than that. Experienced engineers, both mechanical and structural, are usually consulted by the architect at the very earliest stages of the design. That is why it is important to have some understanding of the problems and aims of the architect and mechanical engineer," she said.

"During the construction phase of the project, we are called on by the contract to interpret what is on the drawings, to offer alternate solutions to expedite the work in the field, and to help remedy mistakes that might be made in the field. It is also necessary to be familiar with the local building codes, and when called upon we must be ready to go to the local building department to answer questions and explain our calculations and drawings."

Kathryn Anner became interested in engineering after working as a secretary for two engineering firms. She went back to school to earn her B.S. degree in civil engineering from New York University. Among her projects is the design of the Tropical Asia Exhibit for the Bronx Zoo.

She attributes much of her success to other women engineers she encountered, and to coworkers and other students. She said, "Once the decision to be an engineer was made, I lost any self-consciousness I might have had about being a woman engineer and settled down to trying to be a good engineer."

RUTH VIDA GORDON

Civil and Structural Engineer

Ruth Gordon presents the story of one of the pioneer women in civil and structural engineering, who is active in her profession and equally active in promoting the rights of other women. Gordon is employed by state government.

Ruth Gordon was the first woman registered as a structural engineer in California. She is also a registered civil engineer.

However, what makes her story more unique is the emphasis she places on the rights of other women and her continuing concern for their career development. She is active in her career, in the feminist movement, and in politics. In addition, she is married and the mother of three children.

Childhood and Education

Gordon described how she selected a career in engineering. "My father, an immigrant from eastern Europe, was a feminist. He stressed the joys and importance of education and mental self-fulfillment. He believed that a woman must be able to support herself and any children she may have since one's future is uncertain and basically one can only truly depend on oneself."

She recalled, "I was a better than average pianist; however, that is not good enough in a limited field. I liked mathematics but had no desire at all to teach. At the time that I was graduated from high school, 1942, one either taught math or became an engineer or scientist. There were no computers then. However, I did not know any engineers, nor did I know specifically what they did.

"Although I had a straight A average in high school, no counselor suggested that I apply for a scholarship. One of my mother's acquaintances, whose son had just been awarded a scholarship, suggested that I apply. I did not even know in which state Stanford University was located when I wrote, but they awarded me a scholarship. In 1943, I was probably one of the first bus driver's daughters to attend Stanford," she commented.

"Because it was wartime, Stanford admitted more women than usual and that first year, fifteen of us said we were engineering majors. The second year there were three of us. After being told that women did not belong in engineering, only two of us graduated, one in electrical engineering, and myself in civil engineering.

"In our sophomore lab courses—forging, foundry, welding, surveying and concrete mixing—the three of us would wear jeans and show up in them at dinner because there was no time to change. This was not done. At house meetings all over campus, it was announced that certain women were improperly dressed. I pointed out that if the university paid my cleaning bills I'd wear proper clothes. A few days later a boxed notice appeared on page one of the *Stanford Daily* that women were to be 'properly dressed' except for those in certain specified lab courses.

"Our biggest problem as women students was that the men had files of old exams and problem sets and helpful upperclassmen in their residences and we did not. So we had to work harder.

"There were helpful professors, though," Gordon recalled. "Among them were Professor Reynolds, sanitary and water supply engineering, and his wife, who 'parented' me, and Professor Oglesby, transportation and construction, whose wife was a professional woman. They were instrumental in my being awarded two scholarships for graduate school at Stanford. This was the first time the scholarships were awarded to a woman. One of the criteria for the scholarship was the expectation that the recipient be successful in the profession—quite something to live up to."

Early Employment

"In summers during the war, I worked at a defense plant as a drafter," Gordon related. "However, the day after V-J Day, a number of women in technical jobs were told either to take a typing job at lower pay or quit.

"The summer before I went to graduate school, I was bombarded with letters from a swimsuit manufacturer who wanted to hire a woman engineer to design bathing suits from a structural standpoint. It was obviously an advertising stunt and the salary they offered was clerical.

"One of the local colleges was offering an instructor's position to a new master's degree recipient. I received an encouraging reply to my letter which I had signed with my initials. When I walked in, I was told, 'We won't hire a woman.' So I made the rounds of consulting offices, most of whom said they would not hire a woman.

"However, I finally got a job with a consultant who was interested in ability and I was put right to work designing a high-rise hospital. I had to move out of town and when I returned, it was a constant process of last-hired, first-fired in the chronically uncertain construction industry. Also, I was generally hired at lower pay than men doing the same or even less-reponsible work.

"I finally went to work for the State [of California] in 1956. There are many professional women of my generation in public employment because civil service is an equal opportunity employer, at least at the journeyman-level," Gordon noted.

"At times, obviously, I have had problems with men and their attitudes and with being alone. However, I have been treated fairly at the State. Because our clientele, the engineers and architects who design schools, are limited in number, they get to know me and my work, and we get along fine. However," Gordon recalled, "many is the time that a man calling the office on the phone has told me that he wants to talk to an engineer.

"One of the things I am having to learn is to deflect anger. The people with whom I deal often are irritated at the State, and they are angry at the regulations. They resent being told that they have made errors. For some, the last straw is that they must deal with a woman. I have to keep reminding myself not to take their hostility personally," she said.

"Of course, there are the lesser annoyances—ladies' events at conventions and sexist advertising in trade journals," Gordon remarked.

Present Employment

"In my present assignment as District Structural Engineer, Structural Safety Section, I am in charge of field observation of construction of about thirty school and hospital buildings. My present territory includes San Francisco, San Mateo and Marin Counties and has an approximate value of one hundred million dollars.

"The agency for which I work is responsible for the enforcement of the Field Act for earthquake safety of public school buildings and the Alquist Act for earthquake safety of hospital buildings. No contract can be let for the construction of these facilities until this office approves the safety of its design. During construction, the district structural engineer has the responsibility for the enforcement of the acts for all public school and hospital buildings in that territory.

"The duties include making such inspections as are necessary for proper enforcement of the acts and the protection of the safety of the public. In addition, there are responsibilities for ordering modifications or changes necessary to secure safety. The district structural engineer must also approve of, inspect and review test results, check for compliance with state regulations, and inspect structural deficiencies.

"I must also review and approve changes, examine buildings for their load-carrying capacity, and consult with and advise engineers, architects, public officials, hospital administrators, enforcement officers, and others with reference to the structural engineering requirements. Other duties include conducting investigations and conferences on enforcement problems. I must resolve differences or carry through necessary enforcement measures, prepare reports, and keep up-to-date on revisions to laws and regulations.

"There has been no difficulty with the contractors or the workmen because I carry the full authority which is granted to our agency by law. Namely, that the violation of the Field Act for public school buildings is a felony and of the Alquist Act for hospitals, a misdemeanor.

"Because I have been involved in outside organizations and activities which have provided helpful contacts for our office, and because I have been willing to take on extra duties, I am being given greater responsibilities," Gordon noted.

Before assuming her present job, she was assistant office engineer. She was the first-line supervisor for ten male structural engineers. In this position, she was in charge of scheduling and assigning projects, projecting work volume, answering questions regarding the laws and regulations, reviewing projects, resolving differences, communicating with design engineers, architects, and school and hospital officials, and keeping current on new and revised legislation.

"Before this I served as a senior structural engineer," said Gordon. "I was reponsible for checking the design of school and hospital buildings for compliance with state regulations for structural safety. I also advised and gave consulting assistance to architects, engineers, contractors, and school and hospital authorities regarding approval or disapproval of the work and interpretation of state requirements," she explained.

Professional Associations

Gordon actively participates in numerous organizations. She explained her entrance into one professional engineering society. "As soon as I was eligible, in 1953, I applied for membership in the Structural Engineers Association of Northern California. It took about a year and some changes in the board membership before I, the first woman applicant, was admitted, although the by-laws said nothing about sex.

"I was later told by a board member that my application ruined their meetings for several months. When I showed up at the Engineers Club for my first lunchtime committee meeting, a waitress informed us that women were not allowed at lunch and so the whole committee had to move. This restriction was just changed about three years ago! The change is due to the activist feminists who pushed for the lifting of restrictions at all segregated clubs," Gordon explained.

Ruth Gordon also belongs to the Bay Area Engineering Council and is a member of the American Society of Civil Engineers. In addition, she is the engineer member of the Advisory Panel for the Board of Architectural Examiners, Examination Revision Project. In addition, she is listed in the *Archives of Women in Architecture* of the Architectural League of New York.

Ruth Gordon gives of her time unstintingly to national and local chapters of the Society of Women Engineers (SWE), and has held numerous offices. "The organizational offices I held provided excellent management experience, particularly being vice-chairwoman and acting chairwoman of the 1979 National Convention of the Society of Women Engineers. This involved management of a very large volunteer undertaking including raising funds, soliciting speakers, planning three programs, tours, social activities, hotel arrangements, and printing and publicity for a meeting attended by approximately 1,000 people.

During her presidency of the Golden Gate Section of the Society of Women Engineers, the section received the California Federation of Business and Professional Women's Clubs Top Hat Award for Outstanding Contributions to the Advancement of Women.

Gordon also finds time to be active in the San Francisco Democratic Women's Forum, the Union Square Business and Professional Women's Club, and the San Francisco Chapter of the National Organization for Women.

Advice to Women

Part of the reason Ruth Gordon is so active in professional groups is that it provides her with a forum for crusading for better conditions for women. She delivers the following message to many groups and associations which have invited her to speak:

"It is very important for all of us to be supportive of each other and helpful and encouraging to other women, not only to the ones who are just starting out but also to those who apparently have succeeded.

"We are so few in number and therefore, so vulnerable, that there is no room for petty infighting or 'queen bee' attitudes. I believe that we are all indebted to the activist feminists who have pushed for sex to be included in the civil rights and equality laws. It is important that we all take an active part in maintaining the gains that have been made and push ahead for true equality of opportunity," she says.

CHAPTER 12

MECHANICAL ENGINEERING

Mechanical engineers design and develop machines and systems. They may also work on the control, conversion, or transfer of energy or power. Mechanical engineers also deal with the methods and materials of manufacturing, where three-quarters of all mechanical engineers are employed.

In fact, probably all large industries employ mechanical engineers. They design and develop power-producing machines, such as internal combustion engines, steam and gas turbines, and jet and rocket engines. Mechanical engineers may also design and develop power-using machines, such as refrigerators and air conditioning equipment, elevators, machine tools, printing presses, and other heavy equipment.

More than 200,000 mechanical engineers were employed in 1976. The Bureau of Labor Statistics reports that each year there are an additional 9,300 openings for mechanical engineers.

In the fall of 1978, 3,811 women composed 7.2 percent of the 52,949 total enrollment in mechanical engineering in United States colleges and universities. That same year, women composed 4.2 percent of the total full-time graduate student enrollment of 4,641 people in this field, according to *Engineering and Technology Enrollments, Fall, 1978,* prepared by the Engineering Manpower Commission.

The American Society of Mechanical Engineers describes the roles a mechanical engineer may play in *A Career for the Future* as work in research or development of designs for building a machine, system, or approach to solve a problem and bring a solution into existence. The solution is spelled out quantitatively and put either into mechanical drawings or equation form.

Mechanical engineer Yvonne Y. Clark worked in this capacity at Frankford Arsenal Pittman-Dunn Laboratory in Philadelphia, and solved the cold-weather jamming condition of a certain ballistic weapon which had stumped coworkers, previously.

Mechanical engineers may also engage in the testing of either experimental research and development devices or the completed machines, systems, or equipment. The mechanical engineer operates these to determine their performance and safety. Yvonne Clark's second job, at the National Aeronautics and Space Administration's George C. Marshall Space Flight Center in Huntsville, Alabama, involved helping to check out the Saturn rocket booster used in the space program.

Mechanical engineers may also be involved in production, finding the best and most economical way of making something. Some mechanical engineers are involved in the operation and maintenance of equipment, such as a central station powerplant, using either nuclear or fossil fuel.

Another role for the mechanical engineer is administration. The administrator in mechanical engineering, as in other engineering disciplines, develops her position after having experience and demonstrating an aptitude for supervising and coordinating the work of others.

Other related fields are marine engineering and automotive engineering. Mechanical engineers may also be involved in marketing and sales, as is Betty Platt, whose story follows.

ELIZABETH PLATT

Sales Engineer

Betty Platt, now a successful sales engineer for the York Division, Borg-Warner, began engineering school at age thirty. She believes this late start allowed her children to get a firm base and gave her the maturity she needed to appreciate her education and achieve sincere rapport with customers.

Early Influences

Platt grew up in the Washington D.C. area, the younger sister of three brothers. She admitted, "My interests were influenced by my brothers and their friends. I came to enjoy mechanical challenges." She once took apart the family piano. However, contrary to the findings of other studies about women who enter engineering, none of Betty Platt's relatives were engineers nor did she know any engineers.

When she was in high school, engineering was not even discussed as an option. Nor did she take any shop courses, because they were not offered. She took only academic courses. She was graduated with an academic major from Notre Dame High School, a girls' school. At her school she was a leader—president of student council and active in French club. She enjoyed singing with the Glee Club and was a member of the National Honor Society. "Even in high school I knew I was a leader. I was always organizing things and convincing people that my way was the best. I knew even then that whatever I did, I wanted to be in charge," she explained.

Besides always being a leader, she remembers always being mechanical. "When things broke, I fixed them. When my dishwasher fell apart, two service representatives told me two different things were wrong with it. I took it apart and found it was not what either man had said, but something else, which I fixed." When she took her blender apart and bought pieces for it, the salesman wished her luck and said he doubted a woman would be able to repair it. This incensed her and made her more determined to fix it, which she did.

She began college at the University of Maryland, but discontinued her studies when she got married. She has two children whom she trained to be responsible and independent. She said, "I know they are proud of me and often brag about me. They frequently ask me how my sales are going." She credits her husband with helping in whatever needed to be done. He is currently finishing up pharmacy school on a work-study plan which allows him greater flexibility to help with the children, she explained.

While raising her children, Betty Platt held a variety of positions. She was appointed a magistrate for Prince William County, Virginia. Prior to that she was a school bus driver, a long distance telephone operator and a service representative for the telephone company. She also did bookkeeping for her brother's business handling the payroll and taxes.

Each of these jobs she credits with helping her as an engineer. As a magistrate she became "prepared to deal with people." As a school bus driver she became unflappable and developed a demeanor that would not permit any foul language. As a telephone operator she used to dismantle parts of the switchboard. As a service representative she was totally responsible for a number of accounts that she established as her domain and over which she had complete control. As a bookkeeper, she learned some of the specifics of the tax regulations and how to keep the kind of records necessary for good organization in business.

When her children started school full-time, "I wanted to return to the telephone company, but they had changed their employment criteria. I would have had to take a series of tests and wait an inordinate amount of time," she said. "I was very impatient and decided to use the time to go back to school. I went to a community college and took a battery of tests telling me which careers and fields I was best suited for. In each test mechanical engineering came out on top."

Education

"I began at a community college to build up my confidence," she explains. "It is kind of scary to go back to college. It was difficult to think I could compete. I would recommend community college to other women so they could get the attention they might need. Things are more personalized there. Because of the individual help that is available at the community college, women will probably get better grades and this will build up their confidence."

After community college, Platt returned to the University of Maryland for two years of full-time study to complete her degree. "As I got into engineering courses, I realized that is where my interest lies. The upper level courses came easier to me."

Just before she was graduated from college, she went on many interviews to see what was out there for her as a mechanical engineer. "I realized I could go into hundreds of different fields: machine design, thermodynamics, petroleum, building design or technical sales.

"I was offered a variety of positions. The final choice was between York and another large corporation. I rejected a lucrative offer in facilities engineering from the other firm. While it offered security and regular raises, I would not have the challenge and pressures that are found in sales. Perhaps when I retire, I might like that type of job," she explained.

However, it is difficult to think of Betty Platt retired. "I am ego-oriented, not money-oriented," she says. "In engineering sales, you can see success right away from your performance. In this place, if you perform, you can see it each month if you meet or exceed your quota. You are paid a base and commission, plus bonus and company car."

Being good at what she does is very important to Platt. She strives to be best, but does not use a hard-sell approach. Instead, she concentrates on demonstrating to consulting engineers and contractors how her company's products will best fit what they are doing.

To learn about the company and the engineered machinery it offered, she underwent a rigorous twelve-week training session. She scored the highest in her class on several tests. After completing the training, she made suggestions to improve its effectiveness for future classes.

Current Position

Betty Platt's job involves a variety of things. "I call on consulting engineers who design buildings and let them know what is new in the field. I help them select and determine equipment applications and hope they will specify my company's equipment in designing a project. Engineers use my skills as a consulting service to them. I also call on mechanical contractors who buy equipment."

Platt performs the majority of the calculations required to determine equipment applications, selects the proper equipment, prepares a proposal, and negotiates the contract. "I bid on jobs whether it is a complete system that will air condition a large building or an individual product for the smallest job. Orders range from $1,000 to $1 million for equipment. A good sale is $100,000. My quota is $450,000, for the first year," she said.

"Since I am the only woman sales engineer in the company, management is waiting to see if I will succeed in a man's world. Yet the engineers are quite receptive to me and respect my professional abilities. The mechanical contractors couldn't be nicer. They call me 'that gal from York,' but they do call me. I have not gotten any negative feedback.

"One of the things this job demands is answers. When an engineer asks something, you have to know how your equipment will perform and fit into the engineer's or contractor's scheme. For example—York's newest product, the Turbo-Modulator, can save owners 30 percent in energy costs per year. The engineer depends on me to introduce the product and provide support with the proper application for the clients. This demands knowing a great deal about your products and your field. It also requires the maturity to deal with people. Because of my sincerity, I have been able to build strong professional relationships necessary for success.

"I also perform a great service for my customers by being available when they have problems. This may mean going to the construction site when the equipment is delivered. I check it out to make sure it is all there and operating as it should be. If it is not, I find out what is wrong and make arrangements to have it corrected. I hope customers will remember how I took care of their needs when they buy their next order.

"I often do go to the construction sites," Platt added. "In the back of my car are coveralls and boots. I remember going to one site of the Metro Subway being built in Washington, D.C. and having to climb down a forty foot ladder. I was scared but smiled and descended.

"Most of the equipment we sell is custom-made and built to order. I have to point engineers in the right direction and show them the complete air conditioning system and how to coordinate it with the rest of the project. I make suggestions on preliminary drawings. For example, with a heat recovery system, popular today, I have some ideas of what the engineer wants and know how our equipment can apply. We discuss the projects. We exchange ideas. We may even do some preliminary sketches on the blackboard.

"This type of meeting pays off. Often as a result of it, not only are the engineers interested in York's products, but they have confidence in me and may call me up to discuss other design problems they face.

"As a sales engineer, my goal is to be out of the office about half the time. However, paperwork and customers' phone inquiries sometimes prevent this," she explained. She does however work long hours—at least fifty hours per week, including one day a weekend. "Nobody leaves at five. You do as much as you want to do, to get a job done," she said. "I am a driven individual. I want a proposal to be just right and will work until it is perfect.

"I had thought about getting a master's degree in business administration (MBA) but with this company, that is not regarded as important. Management in sales is more marketing, a people job, rather than a financial job. The sales manager directs us to manage our time, helps develop our selling strategies, and trains new sales engineers.

"This job is exciting because I get to meet half of the engineers and mechanical contractors in the city. I have already had job offers from several of the engineers with whom I have dealt. They have seen my abilities and would like me to work with them directly.

"I am happy with York and I expect to be recognized and rewarded for my work here. I finished about 70 percent over my quota the first year. In the future I expect to be a district sales manager, but my ambition does not stop there," she noted.

Professionalism

Betty Platt believed that in order to do the best job, she should become a professional engineer. To do this, she had to be an Engineer in Training

(EIT) for four years. To become an EIT you must take tests which cover all basic engineering skills: mechanical, chemical, and electrical. After four years of professional experience, you are eligible to take the Professional Engineer (P.E.) exam in your chosen discipline.

When dealing with professional engineers, a sales engineer gains added credibility if she is also a P.E. The trend today is toward more licensure. Having the P.E. is another stamp that says, "Yes, I am a professional." Some jobs require you to have the P.E., but technical sales does not.

As another facet of her professionalism, Platt is a member of the National Society of Professional Engineers (NSPE), an interdisciplinary engineering group. She is also State Guidance Coordinator for the Virginia Society of Professional Engineers. The purpose of this committee is to bring engineering to schools and communities and to provide professional representatives at career workshops and classes. She believes it is important to let the community know what engineers do.

It is important to get engineers involved in their own communities, Platt believes. In Platt's small office is a picture of Jacques Cousteau standing next to her. Cousteau in an address to NSPE said, "Think globally, act locally." "In order to preserve our oceans, we must start with our streams," Platt said.

"Often lawmakers make decisions on technical topics without understanding the ramifications of their decisions. It is important for every engineer to make a community contribution," she said. For example, she pointed out that in West Virginia there is a suspension bridge that should be preserved. NSPE is encouraging the preservation of this landmark.

Women in Engineering

Betty Platt has much to say on women in engineering and the problems they may face. In college she decided she would rather join the general professional societies than the Society for Women Engineers since SWE concentrated its efforts on the problems of women rather than on the profession.

However, she admitted, there are sometimes jibes from her male peers like "'If you are working overtime, the kids aren't going to get any dinner.' They would never say anything like this to any of the men engineers working late," she said.

Platt conceded that men often react differently when there is a woman around. On one occasion, her male boss took her along to a meeting with another man, a client who was known to be abrasive. When the client saw her, his attitude softened and the meeting went on amicably.

"I expect the men I come in contact with to respect me and to watch their language. Women should not have to adapt to men's situations. I expect men to act professionally whether men or women are involved.

"Another potential problem involves dealing with other women in the office who may be unaccustomed to working with professional women. But developing good working relationships always takes time and patience from all.

"Despite these drawbacks, I have done quite well in my position and have received an outstanding review from my manager. I have learned that you don't have to like everyone, but you must learn to work together professionally."

Betty Platt believes that most women do not choose to be in engineering sales because "you must be aggressive, extremely self-confident and have a big ego as well. The job is filled with uncertainties but it also has its challenges. I had to prove that I could do it," she said.

She offered the following advice to other women considering a career in engineering: "Try any career you want, whether you are sure you can succeed or not. If you don't succeed, you find out more about yourself and this self-realization can only help you in the future," she concluded.

JUDY G. DRIGGANS

Solar Engineer

Judy Driggans is a new engineer who works for a public utility doing research on solar technology. She explained her position this way. "My job at the Tennessee Valley Authority (TVA) involves monitoring the development of specific solar technologies. These include work with solar photovoltaics, solar ponds, and satellite power systems and recommending TVA involvement, where appropriate. Being familiar with these solar technologies, I also prepare responses to the public on requests for information and on energy-related inventions.

Early Interests and Education

"I became interested in mechanical engineering during my second year at the University of Tennessee, where I earned my Bachelor of Science degree in mechanical engineering in 1978. I started out in a new program called Applied Math which had three options: computer emphasis, business, or engineering. I chose the engineering emphasis.

"As I took the engineering courses, I became more interested in an engineering career. Also, the job opportunities after graduation looked better in an engineering field. During college I worked for TVA in the Power Production Division, where I assisted in standard tests of coal-fired boilers."

Immediately after school, Driggans took her Engineer in Training (EIT) exam. In several years she will be eligible to take the Professional Engineer exam to become a licensed professional engineer.

"I have not experienced any unique problems due to my sex," Driggans commented. "At the University there seemed to be some pressure on the female students to excel to prove to the male students that we were serious about our careers. The fellows were all aware of the push to hire minorities and they resented this close to graduation," she explained.

Judy Driggans is a member of the Chattanooga Engineers Club and co-chairperson of its Special Projects Committee. The Special Projects Committee arranges tours for the club to keep its members informed of new developments in the city.

Advice to Other Women

She offered the following advice to young women contemplating a career in engineering: "Always do your best. The world is watching you and awaiting your input in the field."

CHAPTER 13

INDUSTRIAL ENGINEERING

"One of the most pressing needs today is for us to find new ways to humanize technology, including the consideration of people (the human factor) during the planning and design of new systems which use modern technology," says the American Institute of Industrial Engineers, Inc. "Industrial engineering from its beginning has been primarily concerned with developing, installing, or improving systems to increase the consideration of human, as well as technical factors."

Industrial engineers are people-oriented, not simply thing-oriented. One of the earliest industrial engineers was Lillian B. Gilbreth, who, with her husband Frank, considered the human factors in industry, medicine, health care, and the home. Lillian and Frank Gilbreth, Jr. were the parents in the popular books and motion pictures *Cheaper by the Dozen* and *Bells on their Toes.* Many of their ideas for time management and "human engineering" received public attention through these media.

According to the *Occupational Outlook Handbook,* "about 200,000 industrial engineers were employed in 1976, and more than two-thirds worked in manufacturing industries. Because their skills can be used in almost any type of company, they are more widely distributed among industries than are other types of engineers in other branches of engineering."

In the fall of 1978, women represented 19.1 percent of the total industrial engineering enrollment of 10,184 people in United States colleges and universities. That same year, 235 women composed 11.2 percent of the total full-time graduate enrollment in this field, according to *Engineering and Technology Enrollments, Fall, 1978,* prepared by the Engineering Manpower Commission.

To solve organization, production, or related problems, industrial engineers may design data processing systems and apply mathematical concepts (operations research techniques).

Industrial engineers may also develop management control systems to aid in financial planning and cost analysis. They may design production planning and control systems to coordinate activities and control product quality. They also design or improve systems for the physical distribution of goods and services.

Industrial engineers are employed by insurance companies, banks, construction and mining firms, and public utilities. Hospitals, retail stores, and other large business firms are increasingly employing industrial engineers to improve operating efficiency and cut costs.

Still others work for government agencies and colleges and universities. A few are consulting engineers. One such person is Margaret Pritchard, a consulting engineer in Portland, Oregon.

During a conference on women in engineering, she described the progression of her career. "Prior to hanging out my shingle as a consultant, I was employed as a plant industrial engineer, working for a national chain of large industrial laundries. Before leaving the company, I was reporting directly to the chairman of the board of directors and president. My business card read 'Corporate Review Engineer.' My job in this capacity required me to visit the twelve company plants twice each year and audit the engineering function of each plant," she explained. She had previously designed the audit system that they used.

After this she entered private consulting. One of her projects involved developing a wastewater treatment system that recycled water for large commercial laundries and some food service industries. She also worked on material handling problems, methods analysis, job description and evaluation, and engineering management and training.

Because the industrial engineer can grasp the working of a total system or plant, rather than just one aspect of it, industrial engineers tend to enter management. In fact, four years out of college, over a quarter of all industrial engineering graduates had entered management. Fifteen years out of college, two-thirds of the industrial engineering graduates were either engineering managers or engineering administrators, according to the American Institute of Industrial Engineers, Inc. (They did not report the percentage of women industrial engineers who entered management).

As we enter an era of belt tightening and increased safety consciousness, there will be an increased need for industrial engineers. The value of such a person is shown by the remarkable career of F. Suzanne Jenniches. Though she received her engineering degree in environmental engineering and works in an electronics environment, the course of her career has been to handle total systems, developing new and more efficient ways to operate.

F. SUZANNE JENNICHES

Industrial Engineer

The atmosphere around Suzanne Jenniches is electric. She is truly a woman on the move. In her five years with Westinghouse Corporation she has moved up fourteen levels in the grade and salary structure of the corporation. She attributes her rapid rise to having a mentor, a plan, and good luck.

"When I came to Westinghouse, I had a mentor-manager looking out for me. My mentor at that time was many levels above me. Now he is only two levels up. He created an environment where I could succeed. He helped me develop a five-year plan. Before I accepted any job I knew the experience a job would give me and where it could lead. I knew why each job was valuable though often others thought certain jobs I took were a step down. Without this plan, I would not have been as eager to take on new assignments because I would not have realized their scheme in the grand plan.

"In a corporation it is difficult to turn down jobs; but if you have a five-year plan, and an unattractive job comes along, you can say that it does not fit into your plan," Jenniches explained with a smile.

Early Background and Education

Before coming to Westinghouse, Jenniches let events shape what she did without her active intervention. She chose her college because she did not have to fill out an application blank for it. She chose her major, biology, in the same way. She taught biology because it was the road of least resistance at the time.

Only after teaching high school biology for a number of years did she realize she was unhappy. So she returned to school at night. She did not have a clear plan of what she wanted to take when she enrolled at Johns Hopkins University in Baltimore, Maryland. Since a master's degree in biology was not offered at night, she thought environmental engineering might be interesting. To enter the environmental engineering program, she had to make up her deficiencies in math.

"In high school I had always been very interested in the sciences but had not especially cared for math. I took an exam in college that exempted me from college math. At the time, this pleased me because I did not think I liked math. However, after taking math courses as a prerequisite to the environmental engineering program, I discovered that I did not like arithmetic but I loved higher math: differential equations and vector analysis. I never knew there was something above and beyond arithmetic," she admitted.

Jenniches received her master's degree in environmental engineering after going to school three nights a week for six years. Based on her experience she said, "People should never feel locked in. They should feel free to move in whatever direction they desire." Jenniches did, and she now says, "Each morning I wake up and am eager to get to work." She did admit that if she were to do it over again, she would probably have majored in electrical engineering initially. "It is better to get a degree in a core engineering field: electrical, civil, or chemical. Then, if you want to go to school to take a few courses and become a specialist, you have the framework for understanding the problems. Specialty fields such as environmental engineering or aerospace come and go rapidly," she explained.

"When I entered environmental engineering in 1970, the field was huge, but when I finished in 1978, there were not as many opportunities. It is therefore better to take the core curriculum and then specialize," she advised.

With a degree in environmental engineering, she could have gone into government-related or private consulting work. She might have worked on the environmental impact an industry had on the terrain or environment, or she might have been doing work on storm drains, she explained.

Career Progression

Jenniches says she was lucky in that during her schooling she met people from Westinghouse who suggested she apply for a job there. She began her work at Westinghouse as a quasi-engineer, a semi-technical position. Once on the staff, the company paid for the rest of her schooling. "For me, working and going to school was super. My husband was very supportive," she explained.

In this job, her title was "product evaluation engineer." She worked for other lead engineers in digital testing, programmed memories, computer programming, and testing of digital electronics, a type of circuit used for storing or processing information, such as in computers, calculators or digital watches.

"Six months later I was put in charge of a project to buy a high speed digital tester. This was a breakthrough for me. Since it was a new field and I knew as much as anyone, I could feel very competent. I researched and bought a high speed digital tester and brought it on line. Within a year I had ten engineers working for me.

"Then I became a project engineer. As a project engineer, I was in charge of capital facilities and test planning for the Product Evaluation Department. I was responsible for the financial analysis of the money used. Previously this had not been a very important job but it was a tremendous learning experience for me. I got to see the complete factory and meet new people.

"At the end of the year, the position was viewed as a very good job. I established procedures and forms to be used by analyzing forms and procedures used throughout the rest of the organization.

"I had a big impact because the company had not been utilizing all the resources that were available. I asked questions that people with more knowledge might not have; I did not see the barriers. I was not afraid to ask dumb-sounding questions. I discovered that people like to help you, to give you whatever knowledge you need to put it together. I traveled to other divisions and brought back good ideas and from all these formed an eclectic package that worked well. I had to have an engineering background to evaluate the project and see its return. I had to know enough to ask the right questions," she said.

To help her ask the right questions, she took two engineering economics courses and another course in statistical analysis and linear programming. These were important to help her learn how to develop ratios and make economic analyses. She did a lot of studying on her own. She worked within the company on her own on-the-job training.

"Formal training provides a foundation, but in my field, which is radar and defense, the work is state of the art. Textbooks on the topic are three- to seven-years behind the time," she explained.

"Before this time no one in Product Evaluation had done what I did, and I brought order to the job. This helped others see its importance.

"Then I entered management as a first-line supervisor. This could have been traumatic because I was going from supervising professionals to supervising hourly operators. I was a first-line supervisor in computer-aided testing. This is the area where I had worked previously. The hourly people knew I was qualified. There were forty-five men on three shifts. Two other supervisors reported to me. There was some friction in the beginning, but it worked out well. The technicians were very good and it was a matter of gaining mutual respect. It was an excellent experience. I was there for nine months and then promoted.

"For the next year and a half, I was a general supervisor and area manager of printed circuit assembly." This was the first job that did not fit into her five-year plan. "Now," she said, "I have to make my own plan. I have to leave the nest and take responsibility for myself."

In this job she had four supervisors and 100 hourly people working for her. "I moved out of the test environment and into manufacturing operations. This also was a tremendous experience. I learned how the radar equipment is built and the interaction of the four other departments. I also learned how the factory works to put a product together and get it out the door. I met new people and made new contacts and friends. It is crucial in order to manage an operation that I have covered all bases so I understand what it takes to get a job done."

She was again promoted to supervisory engineer in the test department. In this management position she has several groups reporting to her: test planning facilities, test visibility, manufacturing research and development, and the mechanical design/hardware group.

"When I took this job, I was warned that the individual who preceded me went out with unparalleled rapport with his staff. I was frankly informed that some people may not be very excited about working for a woman or me in particular because I already had a reputation for moving around a lot.

"Yet," she said, "the response of these sixteen people has been tremendous. The group has done very well. Because I had other experiences, I am aware of all the options. I try to help others advance in their careers as well. I take key individuals of my group to meetings and try to open up new options for them. I am very happy with this job.

"In my current job there is not a whole lot of growth for me. So I am already developing a replacement for me. This is important," she explained, "because if you are good, you may be found to be irreplaceable. It is important to me to keep moving and if an offer comes along and I have groomed a replacement, then I am free to accept it. If an offer does not come along and there is someone ready to assume your position, this person might be able to take another good offer. Developing my replacement helps me build support from my people. In management, you must delegate, because your success depends on what improves the corporation overall."

Suzanne Jenniches was recently promoted again. She began working on the project she will head as part of a blue-skies research and development program. She had had the opportunity to develop this concept with the aid of upper management and submitted a proposal to the Corporate Productivity Improvement Committee for funding. It was accepted. She will be working with a special team on a brand new way of manufacturing printed circuit assemblies.

This project presents much opportunity to travel and develop the new process technology. She recently returned from two and a half weeks in Japan on a series of technical exchanges with major electronics companies who are pioneering new manufacturing techniques.

Ms. Jenniches admitted, "Entering my new position is sort of scary. It parallels how I felt about leaving teaching. It was very agonizing going from a secure, tenured job to an unknown job. I wondered then what am I going to do in a defense plant?"

She quickly found out. Now she believes that this company provided her with a secure, relatively low risk, very logical progression. Her new job is an abrupt change. "I am a little apprehensive. We'll see if this will work out." It is a three- to five year project—three years to initiate and the rest of the time for implementation in the factory.

"Over the long term, I would like to manage a division. This is parallel to managing a small company. By small," she said, "I mean a company that does business on the order of $5 to $10 million a year.

"I am very happy with Westinghouse. Yet, I would have no hesitation about leaving as long as there were no further opportunities for growth here. I like my job a lot. And I guess I could be classified as a 'company man.'

"I also want to stay with a large company. In a large company there are many avenues up and many different kinds of products with which to work. A small company might be more rigid in its hierarchy and progression might be slower.

"I like to take risks when I feel the odds are in my favor. I don't like to gamble, so I work hard to be knowledgeable enough to assess the degree of risk involved," she said.

Professional Societies

Jenniches also thrives on challenges. She assumed the presidency of the Baltimore-Washington Chapter of the Society of Women Engineers at a time when the society was largely inactive. "I want to get it back in action. Its purpose is to make young women aware of careers in engineering and options available and to provide role models. It also serves as a network of women engineers to call on and assist one another in their upward mobility," she explains.

Jenniches also belongs to the Institute of Environmental Sciences and is a member of the Engineering Affairs Committee of the American Association of Engineering Societies. She has recently joined the Institute of Electrical and Electronics Engineers (IEEE).

"Most of my free time I give to Westinghouse," she noted, "giving tours and presenting papers at conferences which can further my technical advancement as well as the corporation.

"Advancement for me comes through participation on the job, not in professional societies. If I can help someone else along the way, I want to do that. Societies are often more talk than action and they take a pedantic, slow approach. I put my energy where I can get the biggest return," she said.

Discrimination

"I don't think I have ever felt discriminated against. I don't go out and look for it either. Many people take innocent comments the wrong way. For example, when I was in the manufacturing environment, one of the men turned to me and said, 'Hey Babe,' and someone said that this was discriminatory. However, he used the term for everyone he liked, male and female. It indicated that I was accepted. You need to look at the total situation so that incidents are not seen out of context.

"To help you see things more clearly, you should find someone with whom to talk who has more experience than you. This person should be someone with whom you work, who sees the environment and who can talk with you openly and confidentially. Thus, a spouse or a personal friend is not always the best person," Jenniches explained.

Jenniches has found such a person in Naomi McAfee, whose profile is in this book.

"The best approach is to talk with the person you trust and find out if you have been overly sensitive or have not seen the situation clearly. Then this person should be able to help you develop and formulate your way of dealing with the situation.

Suzanne Jenniches described herself as "aggressive, bull-headed, and stubborn. In a business decision, if I believe I am right, I will fight to the end. I have a hard, pragmatic business approach. I talk with people in an outspoken way. Then when it is ended, I wipe the slate clean and we are friends again. I don't take business decisions personally. In dealing with people I try to be open and friendly, and as warm as I can be," she said.

Advice to Women

For women considering a career in engineering, she recommends that they enter electrical engineering, especially programs with a heavy emphasis on computer programming. Persons who have a degree in electrical engineering with data processing, hardware coupled with software, can almost name their own salary.

"Everything is now being done electronically. Electronics set up data files and retrieval. Even if you don't have a degree in data processing, you must know enough to ask the right questions. If a programmer tells you something can not be done, this is rarely true. With enough time and money, it can be. I want to have the ability to decide whether it is worth the time and money to do something. Also, if a programmer gives me an estimate of the time and money, I must have enough knowledge to know if the estimate is accurate. Data processing is the key to the future."

Suzanne Jenniches should know. She is in the vanguard of the future.

Overleaf: Nancy Sobczak is a systems engineer, private pilot, scuba diver and family woman who also enjoys fashion design, skiing, and other hobbies.

CHAPTER 14

SYSTEMS ENGINEERING

Systems engineering concerns the relationships among parts of a complex organization. This organization may involve people and machines and their relationship to the social and physical environment. It may involve electrical, fluidic, thermal, mechanical, chemical, and other parts which work together within a system, such as an aircraft, power, computer, automobile, or mass transit. Systems are investigated by modeling, simulation, and a variety of mathematical methods.

A systems engineer may be trained in almost any branch of engineering, including systems engineering itself.

In the fall of 1978, 146 women composed 18.1 percent of the 808 undergraduate students enrolled in systems engineering in United States colleges and universities. That same year seventy-five women made up 13 percent of the 575 full-time graduate students enrolled in this area, according to *Engineering and Technology Enrollments, Fall, 1978,* prepared by the Engineering Manpower Commission.

Dr. Lynne Holt, an assistant professor of civil engineering at Princeton University, is interested in a variety of systems engineering projects, according to an article in *The University: a Princeton Quarterly.* "One study concerns air traffic control communications and collision risk analysis. Information from this work might be used to set new navigational standards for air transportation." Dr. Holt has also worked on energy resources management—how to allocate energy resources so they are not wasted and are used with maximum efficiency and minimum costs.

Nancy Sobczak, whose story is in this section, is responsible for providing technical leadership in the design and development of both hardware and software for her company.

NANCY LANING SOBCZAK

Systems Engineer

Since 1973, Nancy Sobczak has been a project leader at Johnson Controls in Milwaukee, Wisconsin. She is responsible for providing technical leadership, and for planning and coordinating the activities of other people in the design and development of standard hardware and software. These designs must meet product requirement specifications and be compatible with both existing products and systems. She also has responsibilities for the data base management systems, and a human factors interactive on-line data base generation system for a complex computer system.

In her current position, her time is divided into four areas: design and development (30%); administration (20%); technical supervision (30%) and supervision of three to five software engineers, and technical consulting with people outside of her group, (20%).

Prior to this, she was a systems engineer for Telemed in Hoffman Estates, Illinois for three years.

Before that she was an instructor for ITT Telecommunications in Des Plaines, Illinois. She conducted classes for customers and engineering staff on assembly language, concepts and programming techniques, hardware, software, and system operations. She even developed an instructor's guide for nonengineers.

She also served as an associate engineer for IBM in Raleigh, North Carolina. There she worked on software development for a supermarket point-of-sales system.

In addition, she has also taught at the Milwaukee School of Engineering, a private school in Milwaukee, Wisconsin. Here she conducted classes in electrical engineering, computers, and biomedical engineering. She also designed and developed a course in Hospital Information Systems.

Education

Nancy Sobczak received her Bachelor of Science degree in electrical engineering and her Master of Science degree from Marquette University, in Milwaukee. She has taken additional course work at several schools.

While in school, she was an officer of Tau Beta Pi, Pi Mu Epsilon, Eta Kappa Nu, and a member of Gamma Pi Epsilon. She was a member and officer of the Institute of Electrical and Electronics Engineers (IEEE).

She served on the Committee on Student Evaluation of Teaching Effectiveness. She also held a research assistantship while an undergraduate. As part of this assistantship she worked on software support for a computer-monitored coronary care unit at Milwaukee County General Hospital. Later she served as a teaching assistant for a freshman engineering course in FORTRAN.

She has had computer experience on a variety of systems and can program in six computer languages.

She explained how she became interested in engineering and systems engineering, in particular. "In looking at various educational opportunities suited to my personal aptitudes, I felt engineering provided the best mix of theory and practical application.

"When I was an undergraduate, I had the opportunity to work on a research project which utilized one of the first mini-computers developed. It gave me a firm background in computers and systems software. It has held my interest ever since."

Nancy Sobczak is married and has a variety of personal interests. She is a private pilot and enjoys flying. She also likes scuba diving, skiing, tennis, and fashion design. Her community interests include the Association of Marquette University Women. In addition, she is class agent for the College of Engineering Alumni Association.

She has produced three radio programs on biomedical engineering and had papers accepted for several conferences, including the San Diego Biomedical Engineering Conference.

When asked if she faced any special problems or barriers in her education or employment as a woman, she replied, "In my education I feel I was given additional consideration and support. Part of it was because of my age—I was sixteen when I entered college.

"In industry, in many respects being a woman in a predominantly male field is a double-edged sword. Many opportunities exist for me because I am a woman and many opportunities do not exist for me because I am a woman."

She offers advice to other women considering an engineering career. "You must be determined to succeed and have confidence in your abilities."

Overleaf: Sally Kornfeld, petroleum engineer, works with a variety of functions in processing low sulphur coal.

CHAPTER 15

NATURAL RESOURCE ENGINEERING

Natural resource engineering includes metallurgical engineering, mining, petroleum, and geological engineering. These fields deal with the location, extraction, processing, and development of mineral resources for products and energy.

The current emphasis on energy independence for our country should lead to an expansion of interest and funding for engineers in this area.

In 1976, the Bureau of Labor Statistics estimated the number of employed engineers in metallurgical engineering at 17,000, mining engineers at 6,000, and petroleum engineers at 20,000. Average annual openings in these fields were predicted to be 900, 600, and 300 respectively. However, current events seem to dictate that these figures were too low.

METALLURGICAL ENGINEERS

Metallurgical engineers, such as Gloria Faulring, whose story is in this section, develop methods to process and convert metals into useful products. There are three major branches of metallurgical engineering: extractive or chemical, where engineers study methods of extracting metals from ores and refining or allowing them to produce a useful metal; physical, where engineers study the nature and structure of the physical properties of a metal; and mechanical, where engineers are interested in the methods of working with and shaping metals such as casting, forging, rolling and drawing. People working in this field are known as metallurgists or material scientists.

In the fall of 1978, women made up 16.1 percent of the 2,542 undergraduates in metallurgical engineering in United States colleges and universities. Thirty-nine women, or 5.6 percent, were among the 692 graduate students in this field, according to *Engineering and Technology Enrollments, Fall, 1978,* prepared by the Engineering Manpower Commission.

In the fall of 1978, women represented 17.3 percent of the 1,014 undergraduates in United States colleges and universities in materials science. Among the 1,023 graduate students in this field, 110, or 10.8 percent, were women, according to *Engineering and Technology Enrollments, Fall, 1978,* prepared by the Engineering Manpower Commission.

Mining Engineers

Mining engineers, such as Julie H. Smith, whose story is in this section, are responsible for economic and efficient operation of mines and mine safety, including ventilation, water supply, power communications, and equipment maintenance.

Mining engineers are responsible for finding, extracting, and preparing minerals for manufacturing industries to use. They may design the layouts of open pit and underground mines, supervise the construction of mine shafts and tunnels, as well as devise methods of transporting minerals to the processing plants.

Some mining engineers work with geologists and metallurgical engineers to locate and appraise new ore deposits. Others develop new mining equipment or direct the mineral processing operations. This involves separating the minerals from dirt, rock, and other material with which it is mined.

Some work in mined-land reclamation and other phases of land and water pollution. In the future, there is expected to be more work involving the recovery of metals from the sea floor and the development of oil shale deposits.

In the fall of 1978, women comprised 8.2 percent of the total undergraduate enrollment of 3,103 students in mining/mineral engineering programs at United States colleges and universities. Women made up 5.2 percent of the 307 full-time graduate students in this field, according to *Engineering and Technology Enrollments, Fall, 1978*, prepared by the Engineering Manpower Commission.

Petroleum Engineers

Cynthia Coleman and Sally Kornfeld, whose stories are in this section, are petroleum engineers engaged in two very different functions for major oil companies. Coleman keeps track of the natural gas reserves and Kornfeld does a variety of things related to the processing of low sulfur coal.

Other petroleum engineers may be involved in exploring and drilling to produce oil and gas at their maximum profitable recovery.

The majority of petroleum engineers are employed by major oil companies and the smaller independent exploration companies. They may also work for companies that produce drilling equipment and supplies.

About three-fourths of all petroleum engineers are employed in the oil-producing states of Texas, Oklahoma, Louisiana, and California.

In 1978, 409 women represented 9 percent of the 4,547 petroleum engineers enrolled in United States colleges and universities for undergraduate degrees. Fourteen women, or 4.5 percent of the 312 total students, were enrolled for graduate degrees in this field, according to *Engineering and Technology Enrollments, Fall, 1978*, prepared by the Engineering Manpower Commission.

Geological Engineers

In the fall of 1978, out of the 1,301 undergraduate students enrolled in United States colleges and universities in geological engineering, 19.7 percent were women. Of the 290 full-time graduate students enrolled in this area, forty-two, or 14.5 percent, were women, according to *Engineer-*

ing and Technology Enrollments, Fall, 1978, prepared by the Engineering Manpower Commission.

GLORIA M. FAULRING

Metallurgical Engineer

Gloria Faulring is a project engineer in the marketing and development department of Union Carbide Corporation in Buffalo, New York.

She explained how she came to her current position. "Through a series of incidents, none of which were planned, my initial work-related exposure was directed at the problems and opportunities in metallurgy and engineering. As a senior scientist in research, my assignments included such tasks as determining the cause and prevention of failures in iron and steel products and improving production processes. This required being knowledgeable in available analytical tools such as optical and electron microscopy and x-ray and electron diffraction," she explained.

"My educational background was in chemistry. In order to become more proficient, I returned to school and obtained an M.S. degree in metallurgy from Niagara University and a Ph.D. in mechanical engineering from the State University of New York at Buffalo.

"Currently, my primary objective is to develop and characterize steels that will meet the growing demand for increased strength and ductility but without a corresponding increase in weight. Energy efficient automobiles and oil and gas pipelines, especially in Arctic regions, are examples where these types of high strength, low-alloy steels are required," she said.

Faulring not only is actively involved in the work at her corporation but she participates in many professional associations where she frequently presents papers. A few years ago, she presented a paper on "Manganese Aluminum Alloys" to the Association of Mechanical Engineers. In 1980, she and two colleagues presented a paper at the Electric

Furnace Conference on "Steel Flow Through Nozzles—Influence of Calcium."

Faulring believes that "since the late 1960s there has been a gradual decrease in discrimination against women. Today, it is nearly nonexistent in the engineering divisions of many industries. For this, we are indebted to the women's movement. Unfortunately, they are not always given the credit they deserve," she noted.

Because of the lack of discrimination and the many attractive features of engineering as a career, Ms. Faulring believes, "for most women considering a career in engineering, the pluses far outweigh the minuses and these minuses will decline as more women enter the field."

SALLY C. KORNFELD

Petroleum Engineer

Sally Kornfeld is a staff engineer for the Pittsburgh and Midway Coal Mining Company, a subsidiary of Gulf Oil Corporation. She presents the view of a new engineering graduate.

Kornfeld explained that her job title "staff engineer," can be interpreted to mean that "I could be called on to do just about anything. I work in the Technology Development group in the SRC-II Division of the company. SRC-II is a coal liquefaction process, designed to convert coal into a low-sulfur, ash-free, liquid fuel source.

"My work is in research and development, but I work in an administrative position, rather than an experimental one. My major responsibility is to coordinate the research efforts of the laboratory in Merriam, Kansas. This involves keeping our Denver office informed of research activities at Merriam and keeping Merriam personnel aware of the efforts at our other research facilities. I help to plan and organize the program.

"In addition, I work on the numerous reports which we submit to the Department of Energy. Since these reports include contributions from various laboratories, a considerable amount of technical editing is required. One recent involvement has been to check the reports for confidential or patentable material."

Kornfeld admitted, "My career path is certainly taking a different order than that of many of the men in this field. I started in an administrative position, rather than a traditional hands-on, experimental job. I have let it be known that I am extremely serious about my career and that I have always been known to shoot for the stars. I see no reason to limit my goals nor do I feel a ceiling exists.

Early Interests and Education

"I would say that I have always been a 'true engineer'. It took quite a while to realize this. I am not sure what sparked my initial interest in science, but I had been considering a career in chemistry or medicine when applying to college. In my efforts to try for the best, I applied to the Massachusetts Institute of Technology (MIT). Fortunately, I was accepted, and soon found that what I had been hoping to find in pure science was actually true of engineering. I have always wanted to solve practical problems which will help ease world concerns. This may sound idealistic, but I am applying my efforts toward one solution to the world energy problem: synthetic fuels."

Kornfeld said, "I had no problems at all at MIT because of the fact that I was a woman. The ratio of males to females was eight to one but I never felt I had to prove my competence. The women in my class competed fairly, and the men had to take us seriously. I never had any difficulties with classmates or faculty. I have heard of others who were given inferior research problems, lower research grants, etc., and these double standards must be stopped. One problem in our department, as in many, was the complete void of women professors," Kornfeld said.

About discrimination on the job, Kornfeld explained: "Though I have felt no discrimination at Gulf, I have had a few problems on the job. If I call other male professionals, they hear a female voice on the phone and assume that I am a secretary. The same thing sometimes occurs when a visitor enters my office. Many times, a visitor has come over to me to check that it is all right to disturb one of my male co-workers. The only real problem is one of professional respect. This is complicated by the fact that I am also young."

When asked if she thought it was possible to combine a career and marriage, she replied, "I have thought a great deal about this. It would take a very special man to be able to understand my responsibilities. Early in a career, it is difficult to say when a transfer may be offered. Few men would be able or willing to move when and where my job may require. I'm not sure where the answer to that question lies.

"Personally, I'm not interested in raising a family, but I think it would be difficult to do in engineering. Engineers do tend to become obsolete if they don't keep up continuously. The field just does not lend itself to several years absence for childbearing. Not many engineers would be in a position to become a consultant—the ideal solution—before their childbearing years are over," Kornfeld explained.

Advice to Other Women

"My advice to a young woman entering the field would be to set her goals high and to keep her confidence up. I'm afraid my advice to her would not be much different than to a young man, except that she must be willing to show she is superior to be seriously considered an equal.

"She should get the best education possible and try to make as many professional contacts as possible. I would suggest that, at least at first, she work for a larger company. This way she could get guidance in adjusting to professional ways," she explained.

CYNTHIA O. COLEMAN

Reservoir Engineer

Cynthia Coleman, pictured on the cover of this book, is a reservoir engineer working for Exxon Company, U.S.A. In her current assignment, she determines the amount of natural gas reserves remaining in several large, complex natural gas fields. Additionally, she designs detailed operating plans for the fields, that will maximize the economic recovery of the resource.

"Typically, I am in my office most of the day in my current assignment," Coleman explained. "On occasion I may visit the field. In previous assignments where I have had surveillance responsibilities, I have spent much more time in the field."

Coleman graduated from the University of Houston in 1971 with a B.S. in chemical engineering. Since then, she has worked only for Exxon.

"I have had some problems in both education and my career in being a woman. However, these were manageable problems that I took in stride to accomplish my goal of being a good engineer.

Coleman is a member of the Society of Petroleum Engineers and the Society of Women Engineers. She is a registered professional engineer.

Advice to Young Women

"Remember that any career of value takes a lot of effort. . . . The career of engineering is a perfect example of a valuable career that offers broad opportunities to women," she concluded.

JULIE H. SMITH

Mining Engineer

In 1979, Julie Smith was named "Outstanding Young Woman in America." Her career proves she is outstanding. She works in a coal mine in Wyoming as a project coordinator, managing and coordinating all engineering and environmental permit activities.

Early Background and Education

Julie Smith became interested in engineering, geology, and mining engineering by participating in school science fairs from the fourth grade through high school. In fact, she was judged "Outstanding" in the Illinois State Science Fair. "My mother encouraged this participation and initially started my interests in studying rocks and minerals," she explained.

At her Freeport, Illinois high school she was named "Outstanding High School Student in America," and also won the American Society of Metals Award and the Daughters of the American Revolution Award.

She attended the Colorado School of Mines, earning her bachelor of science degree in geological engineering in 1976. During college she gained experience in petroleum geology with a local consulting company, and she did some geological engineering for the Illinois Gas Company. She also did some exploration geology in small underground gold and silver mines in Colorado.

Career Progression

Immediately after graduation from college she began working for Gulf Mineral Resources Company in the engineering services department as a mining engineer. "I gained a wide variety of experience in project evaluation, coordination, and development," she explained.

"Specifically, I have been involved with designing drilling programs, reserve estimations, feasibility studies, mine planning, and environmental permitting work. Most of my work at Gulf has centered around coal resources (both underground and surface mining projects), although I have worked with uranium and phosphate reserves as well," she explained.

Last year she was promoted to the position of project coordinator. She also serves as Pittsburgh & Midway Coal Mining Company's representative on Gulf's Research and Development Technical Advisory Committee for Underground Coal Gas Function. The Pittsburgh & Midway Coal Company is a subsidiary of Gulf Oil Corporation.

She explained what it is she does on her job. "Basically, I am involved with the development of coal and other mineral resources from the very late stages of exploration through mining production. I define the quantity and quality of mineral reserves through drilling, evaluate the economic potential of a reserve, and design a mining plan for surface or underground mines. I then develop the required environmental permits which enable a company to begin mining. I become involved with all facets of project development such as land acquisition and marketing," she said.

"Advancement," she explained, "can normally occur in one of two directions. One method is by working in the field at a mine and progressing to a mine manager's level. Another route is to work in project-design evaluation and progress to the managerial level of an engineering department."

When asked if she faced any problems either in her education or on the job because she is a woman, she replied, "A woman faces problems daily whenever she is involved in a predominantly male occupation.

"People cannot be expected to change cultivated ideas with regard to male and female roles overnight. However, if I believed what people said about women not belonging in mining, then the possibility for change would never occur and many people would be unfulfilled.

"Personally, I believe that these difficulties have been a great challenge and have contributed to my growth and strength as an individual. If something is easy, there probably isn't very much to be gained from it. I think the most exciting part of my work is the challenge of trying to alter people's ideas and have them develop some respect for me as a professional."

Smith believes that it is possible to combine a professional career with a husband and family, but that "this is never easy. It is important to establish yourself as an individual with certain priorities, goals, and a semi-stable career position before marriage. I think a marriage can work in this situation but both people must be very supportive of one another and very much aware of the constraints on an individual's time.

Advice to Women

For young women considering a career in this field, she offered the following advice: "First of all, be very sure that you want to be an engineer. You should always work harder than anyone else. Always be aware of the fact that people are scrutinizing you much more closely than other people in your profession. And never expect or accept any special favors or considerations. Don't expect everyone to like you, but earn everyone's respect. Always remember that you will be a stronger individual if you survive difficult situations and overcome hardships. Your reward will be the respect of your peers," Ms. Smith concluded.

Overleaf: Nancy Nicholas, environmental engineer, began experimenting with mechanical and electrical engineering projects as a child. She loves environmental engineering, and says "You can't beat it" as a career.

CHAPTER 16

ENVIRONMENTAL ENGINEERING

Nearly any area of engineering may be used as a base for environmental engineering, or a person may major in environmental engineering itself. The specific areas an environmental engineer addresses include the development of pollution control devices, materials, and processes compatible with the environment. Some of the career areas include monitoring and controlling air and water pollution; sewage treatment, including recycling, and disposal; surveying and mapping; industrial waste disposal; and the growing area of industrial hygiene.

Nancy Nicholas, whose story follows, describes how her love of water led her to become an environmental engineer. F. Suzanne Jenniches, whose story is in the section on industrial engineering, was also trained in environmental engineering.

In the fall of 1978, 268 women made up 19.5 percent of the total undergraduate enrollment of 1,373 in environmental engineering in United States colleges and universities. Of the 844 full-time graduate students in this area, 110, or 13 percent, were women, according to *Engineering and Technology Enrollments, Fall, 1978,* prepared by the Engineering Manpower Commission.

NANCY NICHOLAS

Environmental Engineer

"Math was always fun," says Nancy Nicholas, a Ph.D. candidate in environmental engineering. "I have a brother three years older than I am. My brother and I always played together. We spent many days taking Mom's appliances apart, building little radios, putting burglar alarms on our room, and working with kits and models," she explained.

"My dad had a tremendous basement and taught us how to use tools and put them away. We spent much time in the basement on rainy days and during the winter. His only rule was not to stand in water while doing something electrical.

"My dad, an auditor for one of the local utilities, thought engineering was wonderful stuff. While both my parents provided general encouragement, they never expressed any preference about what I did. It was important for me to make my own decisions. My mother still has reservations about engineering as a career for me. I think she would prefer to see me raising kids rather than back in school. Yet, she seems genuinely proud of the fact that her daughter is an engineer.

"My uncle is an engineer, but I did not realize that this was what he did until I was in college. I did not know anyone who had gone into engineering," she said.

Education

"In high school I was interested in math and physics, but I knew I did not want to teach," she explained. "I wanted more of an application of my knowledge.

"My high school physics teacher suggested that I might try engineering. I hadn't thought of it before," she said. In high school she was in the accelerated math program and captain of the high school math team. Then she took physics and realized that this was functional math. She could see the way things moved and what they did. "Engineering," she reasoned, "was mid-point between math and physics."

However, her high school guidance counselor tried to discourage her from becoming an engineer because young women don't do it, she was told. She did not take any shop courses or drafting courses for this reason. So without much guidance, she recalls, "I randomly applied to colleges that looked interesting and ended up at Swathmore because it was a nice, small liberal arts and engineering school.

"When I entered college, I was still not positive that I wanted to go into engineering. I took the first-year core-program and then entered the civil engineering program. I realized that civil engineering was not what I wanted. I felt that environmental engineering was much more in line with my interests but it wasn't offered.

"So for a year I dropped out of the engineering program entirely and took courses in Eastern religious studies and biology. The next year, I constructed my own program in environmental engineering by taking ecology and environmental courses in the civil engineering department, plus related courses in biology, chemistry, and geology.

"Swarthmore was a liberal college. I got lots of support and did not encounter any sex discrimination. There were seven women and twenty-three men in my class.

"My college career counselor believed that as a woman I would not have any problems finding a job. While this may have been basically true, I needed help in deciding where to look for the kind of job I wanted, rather than counseling in how to get hired.

"I got a lot of suggestions from people in my school's engineering department. They were a wonderful bunch of guys, always willing to lend support to students. Their general enthusiasm and encouragement was what brought me back to engineering and caused me to pursue it after college."

Career Progression

"The first place I applied for an engineering job was with the federal government. [The federal government hires more engineers than any other employer.] I ran into a lot of trouble here. I was not considered an engineer because I had come through a non-standard route. I learned this when I first tried to get a Civil Service job. Civil Service (now called the Office of Personnel Management) has standards for those who seek to get on the engineering register. The register is a list of people who are eligible for government engineering jobs. Inclusion is based on having completed a specified list of courses. I could not get on the register because of discrepancies between the catalog descriptions of courses I had taken and what the Civil Service employment officer expected.

"I did not know what kinds of jobs were available in my field, but I reasoned that a consulting firm, which worked on many contracts, would provide me with a wide exposure to a variety of experiences. So I answered want ads in the paper from consulting firms.

"I accepted a job with an environmental consulting firm in Reston, Virginia, where I worked for more than a year. It was a branch of a larger company, tightly managed by one man. I was hired along with two other men with comparable degrees who each received $2,000–$3,000 more than I did. I rationalized that they had summer experience at work that I lacked. When I joined this firm, there were three other professional women on the staff of twenty-five. I later learned that the women were the lowest paid of all the professionals.

"I was not prepared for this type of blatant discrimination. Coming out of a liberal educational program, I simply did not expect to run into this type of problem. At first I thought I was having problems because I was overly conscious of being a woman in the company. Despite the difficulties, the job did enable me to gain experience working on a variety of projects and with a variety of federal agencies. Now, I am glad that I did not get my first job with the federal government. Consulting gave me a much greater exposure to the range of jobs open to me in my field.

"One of the contracts I worked on was for the Environmental Protection Agency (EPA). My job was to design a computer-storage system on water quality. It would target pollutant dischargers as well as chemical pollutants and help EPA build up a data file. Data collected was transferred into computer-readable form to handle tissue, sediment, and water quality data. Based on this input, the computer would generate maps showing the location of different pollutants. It would tell where the pollutants were and associate them with the discharges from different industries.

"When I was working on the EPA project, I had no programming experience except for some brief work at school. At the end of the job, I wound up supervising six others. I was originally hired to handle all this alone until the success of the task prompted an expansion of the contract. This made the work impossible to complete alone. So when the contract was expanded to pay for others, I moved from hands-on work to administration and management.

Nicholas admitted, "I tended to get frustrated in this management position because I saw what the other people were doing and I knew it would often have been easier to have done it myself. However, there simply was not the time to do it."

After this project was completed, she worked on a contract for the Army Corps of Engineers. It was a state-of-the-art review of the characteristics of wetlands. Wetlands are those areas, such as marshes or bogs, which are under water 80 percent of the time and have much vegetation. "I assessed the significance of wetlands as well as ground water filters and recharge areas, and examined the environmental consequences of disturbing or eliminating wetland areas," Nicholas explained.

Most of the contracts were short term, so she had many different experiences. "I participated in several contracts that required visiting agencies and going out in the field. Sometimes, when I walked into a conference room, the others there assumed that I was a secretary. Eyebrows were raised when they learned I was the engineer who would help them with their project.

"One of the more interesting short-term conferences I attended was given by the Nuclear Regulatory Commission. It was a workshop for state representatives. I would sit in on the work group, take notes and answer questions.

"Despite the good times, I still felt tense at my job, and seeing little opportunity for advancement, I decided to switch jobs. I heard about and applied for an internship at the Congressional Budget Office's

Natural Resources Office. I worked there for nine months till I went back to school full-time. On this job, I wrote a policy paper on water constraints to the development of oil shale industries in the west. I did another paper analyzing proposed cost-sharing legislation on water projects.

"After trying my hand at a number of jobs related to environmental engineering and policy, I realized that my interests were focusing on water resource-related issues," Nicholas explained.

"I decided to return to school for more specific training in this area. I felt that while my background was broad in many sciences, it was lacking in economics, modeling and the kind of training where I could combine engineering and policy analysis.

"In addition to these academic reasons for returning to school, I was aware of other benefits an advanced degree would bring," Nicholas said. "To continue in consulting, an advanced-degree would represent the expertise necessary to qualify for a greater number of jobs. In a proposal, a bidder includes resumes of key staff who would work on a contract should the company be awarded it. Part of the judging of a company's fitness to handle a particular contract is based on the background and qualifications of the staff.

"I also decided to get on the professional engineering register. This requires sitting for a test on all facets of engineering and after a specified period of time, taking another test in my particular area. The Professional Engineer (P.E.) is another indicator of qualifications and in many instances can also mean a sizable increase in pay or position," Nicholas said.

"At first I went back to school part-time at night but I dropped out because the university courses I took were too abstract. The courses focused on highly mathematical models but I was looking for something applied. I found what I wanted at Johns Hopkins University in Baltimore. Their program of geography and environmental engineering focuses on water resources. The department is small. About one third of the students enrolled are women. However, I am the only woman with an engineering background. The other women have backgrounds in chemistry or other sciences. After another year of course work, I hope to write my Ph.D. dissertation. In this program you go directly from your bachelor's degree to your Ph.D."

As to her future plans, Nicholas says she would like to work in policy-related areas. "However," she notes, "resource-policy analysis with a technical background might get boring after a while. I would like to combine it with hands-on work. Ideally, I would like to work for a planning agency on supply planning and water management. Staying on the lower level of government would probably keep me closer to hands-on work," she said.

Nicholas chose environmental engineering for several reasons. She chose engineering itself because she knew she could always get a job while she saw many of her friends with liberal arts degrees and no jobs. She chose environmental engineering because she always loved the water. She recalled, "My family had a cabin cruiser and for years we spent weekends and summers on the Potomac River." So she chose a field where she could combine her love for the water with engineering. "It is interesting and fun, too. You can't beat it," she emphasized.

Advice to Other Women

She offered this advice to other women considering a career in engineering: "Engineering is a good field for women. In many schools and government agencies there is reverse bias. It is easier for women to get in and go farther when they get out of school. Engineering is one of the few areas where you do not necessarily need a graduate degree. Additionally, it is fun. It's a field with lots of room for creativity.

"As a consultant," she believes, "Once you have established yourself and have experience, you have the flexibility to tailor your own schedule and have time to work around a family." One of her friends, a partner in an environmental consulting firm, is writing a residential water conservation manual for the Department of Housing and Urban Development while raising children and working around her family's schedule at home.

Nicholas believes that jobs in the 1980s will increasingly focus on environmentally-related engineering issues. "Water resources is becoming a more popular area."

Outside Interests

Outside of her work and school, Nancy Nicholas enjoys refinishing furniture. She also throws pottery on the wheel. She does a lot of knitting and handiwork. In the house she occupies, she has stripped floors, built many things and put in a new closet. "I like to putter. There is always a lot of fun in doing things like that," she concluded.

Overleaf: Janet M. Embrey inspects a cell stack assembly of thermal batteries used primarily in military applications.

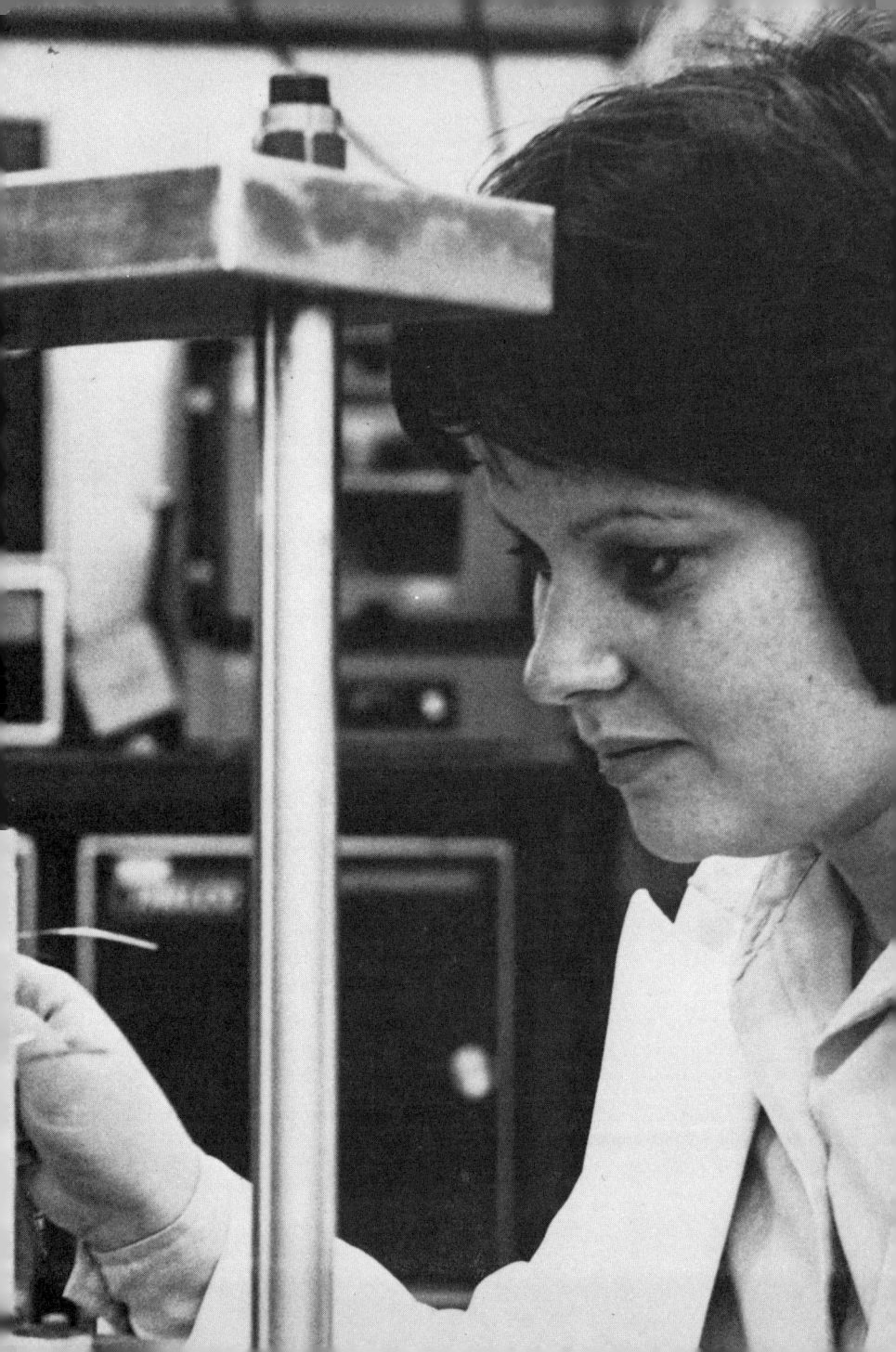

CHAPTER 17

OTHER ENGINEERING AREAS

Women are now participating in every engineering discipline. Some of the areas of engineering which are not discussed elsewhere in this book include agricultural engineering, ceramic engineering, computer science, nuclear engineering, engineering science, and general engineering.

AGRICULTURAL ENGINEERING

Agricultural engineering is the principal engineering discipline which serves the agricultural industry. It is concerned with providing food and fiber for people. To do this involves inventing machines, chemicals, and materials to handle the equipment products, and services in a cost-effective and safe way.

Because of the increasing demand for agricultural products, this area of engineering is expected to grow. New agricultural engineers may help modernize farm equipment, and improve conservation of resources, use of agricultural products, and proper disposal of wastes.

In the fall of 1978, 249 women made up 8.2 percent of all full-time undergraduate students enrolled in agricultural engineering in United States colleges and universities. Eighteen, or 3.3 percent of the 551 full-time graduate students enrolled in this field, were women, according to *Engineering and Technology Enrollments, Fall, 1978,* prepared by the Engineering Manpower Commission.

CERAMIC ENGINEERING

Ceramics include all nonmetallic inorganic materials which require the use of high temperatures in their processing. This includes glassware, heat-resistant materials for furnaces, electronic components, and nuclear reactors.

Ceramic engineers design and supervise the construction of plants and equipment that manufacture these products: whitewares, such as porcelain and fine china dinnerware; high voltage electrical insulators; structural materials—brick, tile, terra cotta; electronic ceramics (ferrites for memory systems and microwave devices); protective and refractory coatings for metals, glass, abrasives; and cement technology or fuel elements for atomic energy.

Ceramic engineering is an area that is growing faster than some other areas of engineering. In 1976, there were 12,000 ceramic engineers employed, primarily in the fields of nuclear energy, electronics, defense, and medical science, where ceramics have highly specialized insulating and other technical applications.

In the fall of 1978, of the 978 students enrolled as undergraduates in United States colleges and universities in ceramics engineering, 19.1 percent or 187 were women. Eleven, or 6.8 percent, of the 162 full-time graduate students in this area were women, according to *Engineering and Technology Enrollments, Fall, 1978,* prepared by the Engineering Manpower Commission.

COMPUTER SCIENCE

One of the fastest growing areas in engineering today is computer science. There are fourteen jobs available for each graduate with a bachelor's degree in this field.

In the fall of 1978, of the 8,632 students enrolled in this field in United States colleges and universities, 1,447 or 16.8 percent were women. Among the 2,488 graduate students enrolled in this field, 403, or 16.2

percent, were women, according to *Engineering and Technology Enrollments, Fall, 1978,* prepared by the Engineering Manpower Commission.

ENGINEERING SCIENCE AND GENERAL ENGINEERING

Of the 5,058 students enrolled in engineering science in United States colleges and universities in the fall of 1978, 764, or 15.1 percent, were women. Of the 1,642 full-time graduate students enrolled, 8 percent, or 132, were women, states the *Engineering and Technology Enrollments, Fall, 1978,* prepared by the Engineering Manpower Commission.

In programs specified as general engineering, in the fall of 1978, there were 52,461 students enrolled in United States colleges and universities. Of these, 7,222, or 13.8 percent, were women. Of the 1,505 full-time graduate students, there were 150 women, or 10 percent, according to the *Engineering and Technology Enrollments, Fall, 1978,* prepared by the Engineering Manpower Commission.

NUCLEAR ENGINEERING

While graduates of programs in nuclear science often have difficulty finding jobs, this is not true of graduates of nuclear engineering. Nuclear engineering involves the release, control, and use of energy from nuclear reactions. The nuclear engineer investigates radiation fields to measure and control the reactions generated. Nuclear power is a growing field for energy. Nuclear engineering is also employed in certain phases of medicine and industry.

In the fall of 1978, of the 2,516 undergraduate students enrolled in nuclear engineering, 205, or 8.1 percent, were women. Of the 1,114 full-time graduate students enrolled in United States colleges and universities in nuclear engineering, only forty-six or 4.1 percent were women, according to *Engineering and Technology Enrollments, Fall, 1978,* prepared by the Engineering Manpower Commission.

APPENDIX

PROFESSIONAL ORGANIZATIONS

The following six professional associations are all located at the United Engineering Center, 345 E. 47th Street, New York, NY 10017.

Engineer's Council for Professional Development
American Institute of Chemical Engineers
American Society of Civil Engineers
American Society of Mechanical Engineers
American Institute of Mining, Metallurgy and Petroleum Engineers
Institute of Electrical and Electronic Engineers, Inc.

American Institute of Aeronautical and Astronautical Engineers
1290 Avenue of the Americas
New York, NY 10001.

American Ceramic Society
4055 North High Street
Columbus, OH 43214.

American Institute of Industrial Engineers, Inc.
25 Technology Park/Atlanta
Norcross, GA 30092.

American Society of Agricultural Engineers
2950 Niles Road
St. Joseph, MI 49085.

National Society of Professional Engineers
2029 K Street, N.W.
Washington, D.C. 20006.

Society of Petroleum Engineers of AIME
6200 North Central Expressway
Dallas, TX 75206.

WOMEN'S COMMITTEES AND ASSOCIATIONS

Association for Women in Science, Inc.
1346 Connecticut Ave. N.W., Suite 1122
Washington, D.C. 20036.

Purpose: To promote the opportunities for women in science and engineering. They publish a job bulletin and a newsletter, and maintain a roster of women seeking engineering jobs.

National Network of Minority Women in Science
Office of Opportunities in Science
American Association for the
 Advancement of Science
1776 Massachusetts Ave., N.W.
Washington, D.C. 20036.

Purpose: To improve communication among minority women in training for or engaged in science or engineering-related employment. Members include more than 200 minority women.

Society of Women Engineers
United Engineering Center, Room 305
345 East 47th Street
New York, NY 10017.

Purpose: Educational service, information and career guidance related to qualifications and achievement of women engineers, professional development to encourage women engineers to obtain high levels of educational and professional achievement. Publications include numerous career guidance materials, national newsletter, and statistical information on women engineers. Membership is more than 8,000. There are regional chapters of this group. Write to the national head quarters for the name and address of the group nearest you.

WISE (Women in Science and Engineering)
c/o Dr. Miriam Schweber
22 Turning Hill Road
Lexington, MA 02171.

Purpose: To provide mutual support and encouragement among women in science and engineering, and to make available information about women scientists and engineers. Membership includes 100 people employed in science or engineering in the Boston, MA area. Publications include a monthly newletter and lists of job openings in the New England area.